John Maclean

LIVES of the LEFT is a new series of original biographies of leading figures in the European and North American socialist and labour movements. Short, lively and accessible, they will be welcomed by students of history and politics and by anyone interested in the development of the Left.   *general editor* David Howell

John Maclean

B. J. Ripley and J. McHugh

Manchester University Press
Manchester and New York

Distributed exclusively in the USA and Canada by St. Martin's Press, New York

Copyright © B. J. Ripley and J. McHugh 1989

Published by Manchester University Press, Oxford Road,
Manchester, M13 9PL, UK
and Room 400, 175 Fifth Avenue, New York, NY 10010, USA

Distributed exclusively in the USA and Canada
by St. Martin's Press, Inc., 175 Fifth Avenue, New York, NY 10010, USA

British Library cataloguing in publication data
   Ripley, B. J.
   John Maclean. — (Lives of the left)
   1. Scotland. Communism. Maclean, John, 1879–1923–
   Biographies
   I. Title   II. McHugh, J.   III. Series
   335.43'092'4

Library of Congress cataloging in publication data
Ripley, B. J. (Brian John). 1938-
   John Maclean / B. J. Ripley and J. McHugh.
      p.   cm. — (Lives of the left)
   Includes index.
   ISBN 0-7190-2180-4   ISBN 0-7190-2181-2 (pbk.)
   1. Maclean, John, 1879-1923. 2. Communists—Great Britain—
Biography. 3. Communists—Scotland—Biography. 4. Scotland—
History—Autonomy and independence movements. I. McHugh, J.
   II. Title.   III. Series.
   HX244.7.M26R56 1989
   324.241'075'0924—dc19
[B]   89-30891

ISBN 0 7190 2180 4 *hardback*
ISBN 0 7190 2181 2 *paperback*

Set in Perpetua
by Koinonia Ltd, Manchester

Printed and Bound in Great Britain by
Hartnolls Limited, Bodmin, Cornwall.

Contents

Acknowledgements

As with all such undertakings, we have incurred various debts in completing this life of Maclean. The Scottish Record Office permitted us access to files on Maclean's imprisonment which are normally restricted and the National Library of Scotland helped us utilise the biographical material on Maclean housed in Edinburgh. We should point out that part of Chapter 7 has previously been published in the Journal of Scottish Labour History. We would like to thank David Howell, for encouraging us to write and complete this biography, and Jane Shedwick, who typed it. In the final analysis responsibility for the content and arguments contained in any book must be assumed by the author or, in this case, authors. It is a responsibility we acknowledge.

Introduction

The past twenty years have witnessed a remarkable revival of interest in the political career of John Maclean. To some extent this is due to the revival of nationalist sentiment in Scotland, where the figure of Maclean provides a talisman and inspirational source for socialists seeking again to find a synthesis between Marxist and nationalist political approaches. Intellectual bankruptcy in the Labour Party and the fading appeal of the Communist Party have stimulated the search for new departures and 'old gods' to personify them.[1]

Interest in Maclean has also emerged from a growing number of academics who have sought to focus on the notion of 'Red Clydeside', the idea that the region trembled on the edge of revolution during, and immediately after the First War, with Glasgow set to become the British Petrograd.[2] Serious discussion of this question or of the relations between the Comintern and its constituent parts, or of the historical role of the Communist Party of Great Britain (CPGB), demands a study of Maclean's part in these events. The results of this reappraisal have not produced an agreed perspective but a further source of controversy, with widely divergent estimates of his significance and of the critique Maclean offered, explicitly or implicitly, of the contemporary political situation of the revolutionary Left.

At the time of his death in November 1923, John Maclean was an isolated figure within the wider Labour Movement as a critic of both Labour and Communist Parties and an advocate of a separate revolutionary organisation for Scotland which could affiliate to the Third International. This isolation had implications for the way Maclean would be treated by posterity. The Labour Party could safely consign him to the margins since he had no political bequests to make to that party. Maclean does, however, appear in some accounts of the lives of Clydeside Labourite politicians.[3] He is generally presented as an awkward personality, courageous in his opposition to the war but compelled by some inner conviction to adopt political positions which Labourites could scarcely comprehend, let alone support.

The political gulf between him and them was intensified by certain aspects of his personality. He was seen as 'very dogmatic and unyielding in his opinions . . . almost completely devoid of sentiment and wholly lacking in a sense of humour'.[4] This characterisation of Maclean as rather dour, prickly and humourless was broadly shared by those who knew him, although it has been overplayed. He did possess an ironical sense of humour on occasion, but undoubtedly Maclean's outlook was overwhelmingly serious and this afforded little room for humour. Even James MacDougall, his long-time political associate, recalled: 'He had little sense of humour, and when . . . he introduced a joke . . . it was clumsily done.'[5] This serious personal demeanour, allied to Maclean's intense and uncompromising commitment to Marxism, led some to think him egotistical and more to see him simply as difficult. It may also have led some commentators to confuse determined political fanaticism with narrow political sectarianism.

While the Labour Party could ignore Maclean, the Communist Party was placed in a more difficult position in coming to terms with his legacy. Maclean, after all, was widely recognised by his contemporaries as the most consistent opponent of the war. This opposition had come to be expressed in terms broadly consistent with Lenin's position of 'revolutionary defeatism'. Among British Marxists Maclean was one of the earliest anticipators of a new revolutionary International and the most vigorous supporter of the Bolshevik Revolution which he urged British workers to emulate. All this brought Maclean to the rather different attentions of Lloyd George and Lenin. On the one hand he was seen as a dangerous subversive, and was sentenced to two long terms of imprisonment for his anti-war activities; on the other he was coupled with Karl Liebknecht, by Lenin, as an example of a principled socialist opposition to the imperialist war.[6] In recognition of his commitment to the revolutionary cause Maclean was appointed one of the Honorary Presidents of the Petrograd Soviet and the Soviet Consul in Glasgow.

In such circumstances it was difficult, if not impossible, for the CPGB to ignore Maclean's contribution to the revolutionary movement. But in the main Maclean was largely ignored by the CPBG, at least as far as official party history is concerned. The problem posed by Maclean was that of reconciling his wartime activities with his trenchant criticisms of the Communist Party formed in 1920-21. In so far as this was consciously done it was through the various memoirs of Willie Gallacher and Tom Bell's biography of Maclean.[7] Certainly they provide the nearest thing to an official explanation of Maclean's political behaviour at the time of Communist Party formation. According to Gallacher, and it is a view shared by others, Maclean's mental health was affected by his prison experience in Scotland.

Thus Gallacher and Bell present Maclean as a heroic individual who suffered dearly for his principled opposition to the war. In essence they suggest that he came out of prison in 1918 with a degree of paranoia which affected his subsequent political career and accounted for his hostility towards former colleagues, especially those engaged in creating the CPGB. It was also used to explain Maclean's apparent conversion to a nationalist perspective and espousal of a distinct Scottish revolutionary party; his so-called 'claymore communism'. It is an allegation which has excited much debate.

I. S. McLean, in his important study of Glasgow politics, has offered the most powerful critique of what he terms the 'legend of Red Clydeside'. He readily accepts the assertion that Maclean's behaviour after 1918 was affected by paranoia; it 'hastened the rift with Gallacher; it blunted the edge of his propaganda speeches; and it increased the instability of his political associations'.[8] Whatever the truth of this view, and it is something we shall return to, it did allow the CPGB to claim Maclean's past whilst repudiating his criticisms of the Party as the product of an unreasonable mind. Maclean, then, was safely consigned to relative obscurity, as one who had contributed to the development of the revolutionary movement but had nothing to contribute to the subsequent debates which would take place within the CPGB and wider international communist movement.

Maclean's memory, however, was kept alive more enthusiastically by a diminishing band of admirers in Scotland. This band included the Scottish Workers' Republic Party, formed by Maclean shortly before his death. This nationalist deviation, which was evidence of mental instability for Communists, was the attraction for those such as Hugh MacDiarmid, the noted Scottish poet and eccentric Marxist, who saw in Maclean the embodiment of a fusion between nationalist and socialist aspirations.[9] MacDiarmid more than any other was able to keep Maclean's name before a mainly Scottish audience, but it was Maclean as socialist *and* nationalist. In so doing MacDiarmid ensured that when the Scottish 'New Left' emerged in the later 1960s Maclean would be available as an example and inspiration.

Until the 1960s such labour history as existed was primarily in the form of memoirs or biographies of participants. The more scholarly work tended to focus upon aspects of Labour Party and trade union history. The history of movements outside this mainstream was virtually ignored. However, at the end of the

1960s Walter Kendall published his controversial study of the British revolutionary movement between 1900 and 1921 which presented Maclean as the undoubted hero of the movement; the lost leader of the revolutionary Left.

Kendall's controversial thesis is that the formation of the CPGB was the product of Bolshevik money and influence and that the resultant party was an artificial creation. The formation of this party was engineered through the person of Theodore Rothstein, an emigré Russian and veteran of the British Marxist movement, who emerged after 1917 as the principal emissary of the Bolsheviks in Britain. For Kendall the resultant revolutionary formation bore the imprint of Rothstein and represented a historic error on the grand scale, cutting off the rich tributaries of revolutionary socialists from the mainstream of the Labour Movement and constraining them within the straitjacket of the sterile CPGB.[10]

In Kendall's account Maclean behaves with extraordinary courage and integrity during the war and is the most far-sighted critic of the 'artificial' CPGB being forged by Theodore Rothstein acting on behalf of the Bolsheviks. The defeat of Maclean by Rothstein in the struggle for the revolutionary Left of the British Socialist Party (BSP) is interpreted by Kendall as the decisive moment in the shaping of the CPGB because it effectively ensured that of the various potential configurations of revolutionary groupings available, it was to be the CPGB which would emerge as *the* Communist Party. Kendall's general argument has been the subject of considerable academic criticism, but it did place Maclean at the forefront of much subsequent discussion about the state of the revolutionary movement in Britain at this pivotal point during and immediately following the war. More recently Raymond Challinor has promoted the case of the Socialist Labour Party as the 'British Bolsheviks' and pointedly questioned the motives of Rothstein falling short of suggesting that he was in collusion with the British authorities.[11]

Specific interest in Maclean was further stimulated by the publication of two biographies written by John Broom and Nan Milton in the early 1970s. Both authors, inspired in part by McDiarmid, adopted a committed socialist approach to their subject; Milton from a self proclaimed Marxist perspective and Broom from that of the non-Marxist socialist. But they both place Maclean firmly in the nationalist camp and thus helped ensure that he would indeed be appropriated by the resurgent Scottish nationalist Left.

If Maclean now came to a wider audience than at any time since his death it was by no means united in its evaluation of his political significance. James D. Young, one of those keen to bring Maclean to the attention of academic students of the Labour Movement, recalled that G. D. H. Cole and Isaac Deutscher dismissed him as an unoriginal and unimportant Marxist.[12] James Hinton, in his work on the Shop Stewards' Movement, has likewise dismissed Maclean's influence on the Clydeside organisation as being essentially utopian and irrelevant. More generally, Hinton has rejected the idea of Maclean as a potential leader of the revolutionary movement. He accepts that Maclean was a 'courageous and able propagandist' but 'the Maclean myth owes less to any achievements than to his fierce and prickly integrity; and to the fact that he was persecuted by the authorities'. Hinton goes on to assert that his politics were 'imbued with a narrow Scottish nationalism which made him unable to take part in the English revolutionary movement'. So in rejecting the claim that Maclean was a viable candidate for the leadership of a Communist Party Hinton uses the nationalist argument as an important ground for disqualification. Indeed he accepts without apparent question that Maclean is possessed of 'this narrow Scottish nationalism'.[13]

I. S. McLean has come to a roughly similar estimate of Maclean's general influence on the Glasgow working class, though for different reasons, and guided by a very different perspective. He rejects the idea that John Maclean can be viewed as a nationalist and states that he is first and always a Marxist. It is precisely because he was such a committed and uncompromising revolutionary that Maclean could make such little headway amongst a working class which might have respected him for his courage and devotion to principle but which did not respond to his political message because it was not interested in social revolution. Maclean, then, is a tragic figure, 'haunted and haunting', who fails because he is ultimately external to the life of the workers he is seeking to reach. This is an approach which is also to be found in William Knox's entry on Maclean in the *Scottish Dictionary of Labour Biography*.

Most recently David Howell, in a study of nationalism and socialism, considered Maclean, James Connolly and John Wheatley as three examples of socialists who had attempted to devise an alternative future using nationalism as the basis of the 'new' route.[15] In dealing with Maclean, Howell observes that any legacy he has left behind is 'a disputed legacy' but one reviewer, Jonathan Schneer, doubts that the legacy is worth much in any event:

> Howell also shows that Maclean was wrong about the potentially revolutionary character of working-class opposition to dilution of labor and to conscription during 1915-16; wrong in discerning 'a spirit of revolution developing inside the workshop' in 1917; wrong, a year later, in thinking he could win election to the House of Commons; wrong, in 1919, when he believed that revolution was imminent . . . Worse still . . . his belief in the social and revolutionary potential of Scottish nationalism. Given all this and with the best will in the world one may wonder what the current Left will find of use or value in it.[16]

The catalogue of failure outlined by Schneer, to which might be added the failure of the Scottish Labour College to develop as the kind of educational organisation Maclean desired does not, of itself, invalidate Maclean's claim to recognition. We know as a matter of historical fact that Maclean's evaluation of the revolutionary potentiality of British or Scottish workers is not vindicated by the fact of revolution, while Lenin's assessment of the situation in Russia at much the same time was.

But it is not clear that Lenin's assessment was any more reasonable than Maclean's at the time it was made. In other words it is not enough to dismiss Maclean because what he thought would come to pass did not, but to ask whether those assessments were so fantastic that they could not be shared by any reasonable body of opinion. Was revolution, for example, something which only existed, at this time, in the feverish imaginations of Maclean and Basil Thomson, Head of Special Branch, as I. S. McLean states, or was it something which affected a wider body of opinion?[17] Certainly anyone who has read the views of officials in the Scottish Office and the observations of senior military personnel can see that concern about a possible revolutionary upsurge in Glasgow was more widely and seriously entertained in 1917-18 than I. S. McLean suggests.

Revolutions are obviously the product of the interaction of complex social, political and economic cross-currents. They are rarely the outcome of simple situations and generally exhibit elements of contradiction. It is always easier to show what did not happen could not have happened in a manner which underplays the variety of outcomes available; complex situations then become apparently transparent. In such a way the Bolshevik Revolution becomes an inevitable outcome and Red Clydeside is relegated to myth. Yet had the revolution in St Petersburg failed, it would be relatively easy to show that such an outcome was 'inevitable'. Likewise had a revolt been sparked off on the

Clyde in late 1917 or early 1918, later historians would have found plenty of evidence to explain that it was a 'natural' development.

At that time the political situation on Clydeside was extremely fluid; industrial unrest was pronounced and social discontent associated with poor housing and food shortages was evident. Military reverses and general war-weariness were reflected in the growing strength of pacifist feeling. The combination of these factors, together with the impact of the revolutions in Russia, gave clear hope to revolutionaries that a major political change was in prospect in Britain. Clydeside was a likely starting-point for such an upheaval, given the presence there of a small but relatively significant body of workers imbued with a background in Marxism.

That this revolutionary possibility did not materialise into a revolutionary fact may be explained largely in terms of the decisive turn in military fortunes. Once the German offensive of early 1918 had been reversed and the prospect of a final Allied victory was realised it is very clear that the idea of a revolution in Britain faded away. In similar fashion the political and industrial instability which characterised the first two years after the end of war and offered the possibility of revolution gave way before the onset of the depression years. But in neither case does it seem unreasonable to countenance the idea that revolution figured on the political agenda, albeit fleetingly.

What follows, then, is the biography of a significant Marxist who was active within the British Marxist movement over a period of two decades which witnessed the break-up of the Second International in the face of a major European war. The Bolshevik revolution and the emergence of Leninism as the predominant development in Marxist theory represented the most serious challenge to the continued existence of the capitalist order in Europe yet seen. In the context of Britain the period witnessed the break-up of the old Marxist SDF/BSP, the emergence of the CPGB and the most serious challenge to the existing social order since Chartist times. When Maclean joined the SDF the idea of revolution in Britain was little more than a theoretical abstraction and Clydeside was firmly in the political grip of Liberalism; singularly unpromising territory for Labourites, let alone socialists. By 1918 Maclean could see Britain entering the 'rapids of revolution, with Glasgow at its centre. Less than six years later Maclean died. Already the left-wing ILP MPs – Maxton, Wheatley, Kirkwood – were becoming synonymous with the legend of 'Red Clydeside'. Maclean, *the* Red Clydesider, was lost from view and 'Red Clydeside' became a journalistic cliché.

1 Becoming a social democrat

John Maclean was born at Pollokshaws, near Glasgow, in August 1879, the sixth child of Daniel and Anne Maclean (neé Mac Phee).[1] Maclean's parents had come come from the Scottish Highlands, moving to the Clyde region as young children; part of the mass emigration from the rural north in the face of aggressive landlordism. This emigration was paralleled by the influx of Irish peasants in the post-famine period. Both these population movements were significant for the economic and social development of Clydeside in the latter half of the nineteenth century.

Daniel Maclean and Anne MacPhee married in 1867 and eventually settled down in Pollokshaws, a former centre of Chartist agitation, where Daniel found work as a potter. The Maclean family were typical representatives of the respectable and God-fearing artisan class, being members of the Original Secessionist Church, a Presbyterian-inspired church which decried the use of any religious decoration such as stained-glass windows or the use of organ music, and which insisted on strict observance of the Sabbath. Although Maclean was to abandon religion, some commentators claim that this childhood exposure to a strict Calvinist regime left its mark on his personality, and may account for his lack of knowledge or interest in theatre or the aesthetic arts as well as his general seriousness and lack of easy humour.

When Maclean was eight years old his father died of a lung complaint common among those employed in the pottery trade. From this point on Anne Maclean was responsible for the welfare of her four surviving children, aided only by her mother. Anne

Maclean was able to maintain her family by returning to work as a weaver, and later by various other occupations. Although their standard of living was frugal, John and his older brother Daniel remained at school beyond the normal leaving age and went on to higher education. In the case of John Maclean he went from Queen's Park secondary school to Polmadie school as a pupil teacher in 1896. In 1898 Maclean entered the Free Church Teachers' Training College where he qualified as a teacher in 1900. He took up his first teaching post at Strathbungo school, under the auspices of the Govan School Board, in whose employ he remained until his dismissal in controversial circumstances in 1915. In that time he taught in four further schools and was often in conflict with the school authorities.

While qualifying as a teacher Maclean began a course of studies at Glasgow University, leading to the award of an MA, which involved attendance in the early morning and evening. In fact Maclean obtained his degree in 1904 and thereafter maintained a keen interest in a wide range of sujects. But above all Maclean had, by now, become absorbed in the study of political economy from a Marxist standpoint. He followed closely the development of current economic arguments and theoretical debates and was well informed about the general state of economic science.

The early Maclean, then, seemed to personify the Victorian ideal of the intelligent and determined young man who advanced in the world by dint of hard work and ability. The profession of the teacher was still, at this time, considered to be secure and respectable and was an acknowledged route for someone of Maclean's background. However, Maclean was already deviating from this Victorian ideal, first by his abandonment of religion and commitment to radical freethinking but more importantly through his conversion to Marxist socialism. This process seems to have started in earnest during his time at the teacher training college and was accelerated by his university studies.

Another contributory factor was his active involvement with a local mutual improvement society, the Pollokshaws' Progressive Union. This Union was formed in 1900 and attracted an assortment of individuals who shared an interest in philosophical and scientific questions. What seems to have united the group was their general opposition to the prevailing orthodoxies of the social, political, economic and religious establishments. Above all they appeared to share a strong commitment to secularism, which influenced the kind of issues they were interested in discussing. James MacDougall was to note later the group's 'special penchant for astronomy because of its supposed anti-God effects'.[2]

Maclean was probably introduced to socialism by Will and Jim Craig, two brothers and members of the Pollokshaws' Union who had connections with the SDF. However, Maclean always said it was through reading Blatchford's *Merrie England* that he was first captured by the vision of a socialist world, a common enough route into socialism at this time. But it was Marx's *Capital* which transformed the whole course of Maclean's life. Perhaps the first public demonstration of Maclean's growing attachment to Marxism was in a letter he wrote to the local newspaper, the *Pollokshaws News*. In this letter he argued that the class struggle was a bitter, living reality for a working class exploited by capitalists and driven to combine in trade unions to resist their class enemy:

> Trade Unions are formed, and the strike is used to get as much of the wealth produced as possible ... Though united, the workers still fight an unequal battle ... Whatever gain is got is soon lost at times of depression, when masters need only threaten the lock-out to reduce wages ... the workers have greater cause for a forcible revolution than had the French capitalists in 1789 ... But the workers need not that method. Their hope lies in carrying the class struggle into the political field, and there they will meet and defeat the capitalists when all the workers see the need for solidarity and for loyalty to their class.[3]

This letter contains key elements of pre-war social democracy as exemplified in Britain by the SDF. The emphasis is on political activity based on class feeling, the recognition of the class struggle, and the ineffectiveness of trade union action as a means of raising working-class living standards in the long term. In this letter Maclean appears to believe that the Labour Party is being pushed in a socialist direction in the aftermath of the Taff Vale decision; that politics is taking on the shape of class-based interests.

Maclean's participation in the wider arena of labour politics took the form of membership of the SDF, but he was also closely involved in the co-operative movement as a member of the Pollokshaws' Society. Precisely when he joined these organisations and in what order is subject to doubt. James MacDougall suggested that Maclean's first public appearances were on co-operative platforms and that he joined the SDF sometime in 1903 or 1904. Tom Bell in his biography of Maclean states that he joined the Glasgow branch towards the end of 1903, a dating which has been accepted by Nan Milton, amongst others, while Broom settled for some time 'around' 1903.[4] All have dated his active participation as a propagandist as starting in the spring of 1904 when he began to address public meetings from SDF platforms. Both Broom and Milton seem to suggest that it was subsequent to his joining the SDF that Maclean involved himself in the co-operative field and Milton cites the end of 1906 as the point when he commenced his distinctive role as a teacher of Marxist economics.

In fact we have established that Maclean was in the SDF at least as early as April 1903 and most probably joined in late 1902.[5] He was active in public propaganda on its behalf throughout the summer of 1903 and was advertised as taking a class in economics under its auspices at the year's end.[6] Moreover he was active as a co-operator at this time and had written to the *Scottish Co-operator* in November 1902 on the subject of municipal trading and the rates. Describing himself as a 'younger socialist', he objected to the profits of municipal enterprises being used to keep rates down. He asserted that all genuine co-operators must acknowledge 'that municipalism is one great factor on our side in the struggle for economic emancipation' and any profits should be used to extend the concept elsewhere. He also urged co-operators to use a proportion of their profits to encourage additional co-operative enterprise rather than become totally pre-occupied with the level of the dividend, citing the case of Belgium where 'workers . . . as trade unionists, co-operators and socialists, use their wealth to spread socialism as well as co-operation, in the limited sense.[7]

In February 1903 Maclean again wrote to the *Scottish Co-operator* in terms which show he was already social-democratic in outlook and make it reasonable to suggest he was a member of the Federation at this time. In this letter he asserted that the Taff Vale decision had effectively crippled trade unions and rendered 'that clumsy weapon, the strike' irrelevant. Maclean argued that it was now necessary to turn to Parliamentary action as one means, at least, of carrying on the struggle against the capitalists. However, he thought this could only prove effective if the Labour Party conducted itself as a self-consciously socialist party:

If labour representation means anything it surely means the action of class-conscious individuals in the interests of that class . . . The uniting force must be class feeling and class interest. To me this seems most practical, because I see how strong, socialist parties on the Continent are becoming. If there are strong, class-conscious parties on the Continent, why not here? Are the workers here too stupid, too ignorant, too gullible, or what? . . . To me it seems tragic that the workers, with rapid trustification on one hand, and the advance of social democracy abroad on the other, do not see the necessity of class policy being the abiding principle of the new economic Parliamentary party.[8]

Our concern to be as precise as possible about the timing of Maclean's entry into the SDF and the co-operative movement is not a case of academic pedantry. April 1903 saw the most serious split in the SDF since William Morris broke away in 1884 to form the Socialist League. This new split was particularly serious for the Scottish SDF and especially for its principal branches in Glasgow and Edinburgh, since it effectively halved the Federation's already small Scottish membership. It is both interesting and important to note that Maclean was almost certainly already an SDF'er and one who chose to stay with the Federation after the split.

Although this 1903 split in the ranks of the SDF has been the subject of other studies it is necessary to say something about its causes and consequences here.[9] Ostensibly the cause lay in a decision of the Socialist International to permit the French socialist leader, Millerand, to join a coalition government based on capitalist parties against the accepted principle of the non-participation of socialists in such governments. What made the French case more emotive was the presence of General Gallifret, suppressor of the Paris Commune and 'executioner' of communards, as one of Millerand's coalition partners.

This issue, which threatened to engulf the International, was resolved by Karl Kautsky who moved, successfully, the resolution which asserted the principle of non-participation but permitted the French case as 'exceptional'. This compromise was supported by the bulk of the British delegates but one dissident, George Yates, returned to Scotland determined to campaign against the Hyndmanite-dominated SDF leadership, seeing the Millerand decision as further evidence of decay within social democracy in general and the SDF in particular.[10]

For Yates this decay was reflected on a number of levels. The willingness of the leaders to consider merging with the non-Marxist ILP and the ballot of members of both groups on the question in 1898 was seen as revealing a lack of firm political principle. In addition the gap between the SDF's theory and practice in terms, for example, of the Federation's tolerant treatment of trade union leaders, was further evidence of weakness.

In theory, trade union leaders were seen as lackeys of capitalism and purveyors of false consciousness, to be denounced without qualification. In practice SDF criticism was often muted and on occasion such leaders were carefully courted. Similar concern was expressed over the emphasis which the Federation's leaders placed on securing electoral success, notably in terms of Parliamentary elections, and the parallel pre-occupation with securing immediate social reforms. All this was seen by Yates and his supporters as symptomatic of a deepening ideological malaise which could only begin to be attacked once Hyndman, Bax, Gorle, Lee, Quelch and the other leaders had been removed.

Between 1901 and 1903 this struggle continued inside the Federation with Glasgow, Edinburgh and London as its main focus, until the dispute came to a head at the Annual Conference in April 1903. Here the Hyndmanite majority secured a mandate for the expulsion of all those refusing to accept the 'orthodox' line with a specific reference to the Scottish dissident elements now identified with Neil Maclean.[11]

In the immediate aftermath of this conference, the Glasgow Central branch met to discuss the ultimatum and a narrow majority voted to withdraw from the SDF.[12] Three days later, on 19 April the remaining loyalists, some twenty strong, met and re-constituted the Tradeston branch to continue the work of the SDF in Glasgow by mounting a summer propaganda campaign and appealing for former members, who had left because of the earlier bout of bitter internal struggle, to return to the fold. This meeting also elected its officials with John Mclean (sic) appearing for the first time as minute secretary.[13] Three months later the Glasgow Branch was formed by merging the Tradeston Branch with such residual members as could be found in the city.[14]

In these circumstances Maclean quickly emerged as a significant figure and throughout that spring and summer was active as a propagandist, often in tandem with James Johnstone, addressing meetings in Kirkintulloch, Airdrie, Cambuslang, and Carlisle, then part of the Scottish district.[15] The main subjects of his addresses were the Free Trade issue and the growth of monopolies, issues which he also raised in co-operative meetings.[16] In addition to the public propaganda carried out at the street corner, Maclean offered a course in economics under the auspices of the Glasgow branch, commencing in November.[17] All this indicates that Maclean was an established SDF propagandist and putative economics teacher before the end of 1903. That he had attained such a prominence in the SDF at this relatively early age – he was still in his early twenties – owed much to his energy and ability, as well as something to the difficult position which the Federation faced in Scotland. Maclean would have been a valued member of a larger socialist organisation like the ILP but to the SDF his contribution was invaluable. Lacking the resources to employ a full-time paid organiser, the Scottish SDF relied on a limited core of activists to 'keep the flag flying'. The District Secretary, John F. Armour, confirmed the Federation's difficulty in supplying speakers to the Scottish branches because of his reliance 'largely on the speakers of the Glasgow branch' who were themselves 'more fully occupied than ever with meetings in the Glasgow District'.[18] Of all these speakers Maclean was undoubtedly the most dedicated and energetic. In most summers between 1903 and the Great War Maclean devoted his holiday to a propaganda tour of Scotland and parts of Northern England: 'He spoke in every quarter of Glasgow, in every industrial town in Scotland from Hawick . . . to Aberdeen . . . and further than Aberdeen, for he addressed the fishermen in the summer herring season at Lerwick.'[19]

This punishing tour of duty was typical of Maclean's summers in this pre-war period but on top of this he was running economics classes during the winter months and acting along with a veteran SDF'er James Burnett, as the Scottish Press Committee of the SDF, monitoring the newspapers, writing letters and generally preparing political material for public dissemination.[20] He was also an active co-operator and a full-time school-teacher. Yet despite this kind of personal commitment the SDF's struggle in Scotland was always an uphill one. In October Stewart Maclaren estimated the membership at 'let us say 200'[20] and in March 1906 J. McNabb judged the spring conference 'easily the best that the Scottish District Council ever held', because the attendance of twenty delegates representing seventeen branches exceeded by four branches and six delegates any previous gathering.[22] The weakness of the SDF in Scotland reflected, in part, the more general weakness of Labour and socialism as a whole. Trade union membership was concentrated on a relatively small number of skilled workers in the engineering trades, coal-mining and shipbuilding. Even in 1900, when the Scottish Workers' Representation Committee was formed, only forty delegates participated.

Against this rather fragile Labour and Socialist organisation can be set the co-operative movement, which was easily the largest organisation based on the working class and which involved women as well as men, unskilled as well as skilled. Indeed the co-operative movement was the only organisation which could be said to be a mass organisation of workers transcending sectional, religious and gender differences and as such might be seen as representing a key audience for socialists. In fact the SDF attitude to the movement reflected something of the ambiguity which characterised its approach to trade unionism. While individual SDF'ers like E. C. Fairchild played a prominent role in the co-operative movement and the Federation officially sanctioned such activity the overall contribution of the SDF in

19

this area was slight, and sustained involvement by individual members unusual. In this sense Maclean's activities as a co-operator were distinctive though not without precedent in Scotland.

The important role occupied by the co-operatives in Scotland as a mass movement of the working classes was underlined by the contrast with the more socially and economically restricted trade union movement, organisations exclusive to small groups of relatively skilled men. Moreover, the co-operatives allowed socialists to participate and to hold important positions. The best example of this was William Nairn, a long-time SDF propagandist who enjoyed a powerful position within the Scottish co-operative movement. In certain respects a forerunner of Maclean, Nairn was elected to the SDF's National Executive on three occasions and was its best known figure in Glasgow, where he 'spent some of the most vigorous years of his life as an advocate of the new labour and socialist cause, serving it alike with . . . uncompromising zeal and unique ability'.[23] At the time of his death in January 1902 Nairn was a respected figure in the co-operative movement, serving as a director of the Co-operative Insurance Society and occupying the post of President of the Co-operative Defence Association, a body which was responsible for ensuring, amongst other things, that the movement's interests were protected in the public arena.

Certainly Nairn was an example of the way in which a hard working socialist could achieve prominence for himself and his views within the co-operative organisation, and Maclean was to devote considerable energy to this same movement for most of his political career.

In January 1904 Maclean participated for the first time at a meeting of the Renfrewshire Co-operative Conference Association (RCCA) as a delegate of the Pollokshaw's Society. This Association was composed of affiliated societies and met quarterly, not only to transact co-operative business but also to hear and discuss papers presented by members or outside speakers on issues of contemporary relevance. These meetings were well attended and it was common for as many as 150 delegates to appear. They were ideal opportunities for socialists to put forward their particular interpretation of events and issues before audiences of predominantly working-class activists.

Although esentially anti-socialist in outlook, the Scottish co-operative movement always provided a forum for those socialists willing to participate in its activities. In the main this opportunity was seized by the ILP'ers who came to enjoy prominent positions in a number of the important city organisations while the SDF tended to adopt a more disdainful attitude, much to Maclean's disgust. Maclean had few illusions about the underlying political character of a co-operative movement which he saw as Lib–Lab, but believed its members might become more receptive to a political message promoting a wider definition of the co-operative ideal. He used the opportunity afforded to try and show co-operators the limits of a movement obsessed with the rate of the dividend and to urge them to see salvation in terms of linking co-operation, both at home and abroad, with socialism.

In effect he viewed the relationship between socialism and co-operation in the same way as he viewed the relationship with trade unionism: both were limited but useful vehicles for building up workers' confidence and as such, organisations where social democrats should be found attempting to raise further workers' consciousness. However, trade unionism was so weak and ineffectual at this time in Scotland that Maclean had very little to say on the subject. It was only after his experiences during the Belfast dockers' and carters' strike in 1907 that he began to consider, more positively, the progressive implications of trade union activity in the development of political consciousness amongst workers.

Maclean always tried to draw out the implications of current issues with the message that only by recognising the reality of the class war and the need for socialism could workers, as trade unionists or co-operators, effectively combat the capitalist and multiple retailer. At the January conference a strongly worded resolution in favour of free trade was discussed. Maclean moved an amendment which recognised that the imposition of tariffs constituted 'a pernicious tax' on the working classes but asserted that

> the adjustment of the fiscal policy to help British capitalists in their struggle with foreign capitalists is a matter of little concern to the permanent interests of the working class; and further considers that the only way of escape . . . is by the formation of a Labour Party, whose object shall be the socialisation of the means of production and distribution, and whose immediate programme shall contain the nationalisation of railways, mines, and lands.[24]

This attracted sixteen votes and was easily defeated.

In December 1904 Maclean wrote to the *Scottish Co-operator* in his capacity as the convenor of the SDF's 'Vigilance Committee'. The letter was in answer to an article which applauded the growing evidence of revisionism amongst continental social democrats, notably in the case of Bernstein. The article argued that continental socialism was becoming less dogmatic about issues like the nature of class struggle under the pressure of changing circumstances.

Maclean's response was to accept that while Marxism was always changing in many detailed ways it remained essentially consistent in its commitment to revolution. Such adjustments as were made occurred because socialism was 'attacking a system of society which is ever transforming its aspect . . . [but] . . . we maintain that the transformation to socialism involves revolution', a term not synonymous with violence. This assertion that revolution did not necessarily mean violence was something which Maclean returned to often. He was at pains to counter the assertion put forward by opponents 'that our struggle for a social revolution necessarily involves murder and bloodshed on our part'. He believed, in accordance with the broad tenets of social democracy, that political transformation depended on the securing of a majority in favour of socialism.[25]

To that end he observed, in a letter published towards the end of 1908, that 'we Britons are units of a political organism. If a complete alteration of the economic condition . . . has to be accomplished . . . a majority must decide. The work of the unit is to create that majority by a legitimate agitation.'[26] This contains a classic exposition of Second International socialism and also suggests that Maclean had no political conception of himself as a Scot. But if he saw the political way forward in terms of 'legitimate' agitation, education and propaganda he did recognise that achieving socialism did imply the use of force and, might, in the final analysis, involve armed struggle:

> To reach socialism, we must take the land from the landlords and the capital from the capitalists. That implies force. If the people have no guns of their own to defend their lives, then the army, dominated by capitalist Parliament, officials, and officers will be used against them. We Social Democrats are aware of this, and therefore advocate the Armed Nation in opposition to Haldane's Territorial Army. The Future alone will decide whether the capitalists will yield quietly or not. Ours is not to trust them.[27]

In the following June Maclean made an appearance as the Pollokshaws' delegate at the Annual British Co-operative Congress held in nearby Paisley. In the run-up to the Congress he inserted a notice in *Justice* asking all socialists attending to contact him, with the object of mounting a distinct socialist campaign on those issues which were of a political character.[28] The most relevant political question on the agenda was the proposal that the co-operative movement should adopt a formal party-political position and affiliate to the Labour Representation Committee. According to MacDougall this set the scene for a verbal confrontation between Maclean and Fred Maddison, a veteran Lib–Lab'er, in which Maclean 'gie'd it to the great man from the south'.

This story is retailed by Broom and Milton although there is no evidence to suggest it is anything more than apocryphal.[29] Certainly the official report of the congress and the accounts given in the co-operative press show that a heated debate on the subject took place, but there is no reference to show that Maclean was even called to speak in this debate, let alone that he fought a verbal battle with Maddison, who certainly did speak.[30] Moreover, some indication of the problem facing socialists of all kinds in moving the co-operatives towards an explicit political stance can be gleaned from the result of his debate. The argument for remaining aloof from party politics was emphatically endorsed by 801 votes to 135.[31]

Maclean did contribute to the discussion on two Congress papers, one on 'Land Monopoly; or Land Values Taxation' and the other entitled 'Is Co-operation Capable of Solving The Industrial Problem?' On the latter topic he voiced his often reiterated view that co-operation could not by itself solve any of the real socio-economic questions facing itself and society at large, but must link up with the wider socialist movement. He also called on the co-operative organisations to prepare for a life and death struggle with the rapidly growing multiple retailers and to start by crushing the small private traders and intermediate capitalists.[32]

Throughout 1905 Maclean worked 'like a charged body'. With unemployment starting to rise, he began to organise demonstrations demanding relief while mounting his normal round of propaganda meetings including his summer tour of Scotland.[33] At the end of the year, with a general election in prospect, he persuaded Tom Kennedy to stand for the SDF in Aberdeen. Kennedy, one of the more established SDF'ers, had been elected to the local School Board in 1903 and so had some electoral base from which to campaign.[33] He actually secured a credible vote of some 2,000 in an election over-shadowed for SDF'ers by Hyndman's failure to win in Burnley.

Maclean's strong concern that the SDF should fight Aberdeen, a town with a radical tradition, was born of his argument that an abstentionist policy was wrong-headed and his rejection of the cry 'a plague on both houses'. Indeed Maclean believed that where it was not possible to put forward candidates for election, some form of manifesto or campaign should be launched so that the ideas and arguments of social democracy could be put before the electorate.[34] However, the immediate outcome of the election results was to emphasise the marginal political position occupied by the SDF, which in turn stimulated again the internal debate about the Federation's future role, especially in relation to the Labour party.

2 Hyndman's gramophone

David Howell has described the Maclean of the pre-1914 period, correctly in our view, as a model social democrat.[1] This presumably means that he remained faithful to the conventional forms of social democratic politics; the emphasis on building a mass open party ultimately committed to social revolution by means of agitation, education and propaganda; the belief in the primacy of political action as the means of achieving social revolution and the consequential rejection of industrial militancy as other than a limited, defensive form of class resistance; and the belief in an international working-class brotherhood which recognised no national boundaries.

That Maclean did hold to these positions is unsurprising in itself, but what might seem surprising is the absence of much which would explain his later enthusiastic anticipation and adoption of something approximating to a Bolshevik political world view. Indeed until at least 1911 Maclean's social democracy bore the strong imprint of the 'old guard' of British social democracy most particularly derived from the 'founding father' Henry Hyndman. On every major political issue, and most minor issues, raised by Maclean between the elections of 1906-10 the influence of Hyndman seems readily apparent. From the question of relations with the Labour Party, the concept of the Citizen Army and the amelioration of unemployment, down to the issues raised by Temperance Reformers and opponents of Marx's Theory of Value, Maclean appears as the faithful advocate of Hyndman's views.

Had he died in 1910, Maclean would be remembered, if at all, as a loyal Scottish Hyndmanite. It is only with the growing debate within British social democracy on international questions after 1911 that Maclean began to break with the 'old guard' of Hyndman, Quelch, Bax and Lee. That breach widened and deepened relatively slowly thereafter, coming to include disagreements on a variety of policy issues and questions of party organisation, discipline, direction and control.

In the post-1911 period Maclean's social democratic model was less and less that of Hyndman than a strengthening commitment to a vision of international working-class solidarity. It is worth noting that Maclean's commitment to Internationalism was based on little direct experience of things foreign. With the exception of one visit to Europe in 1909 shortly before his marriage Maclean seems never to have left the British Isles. Indeed before 1918 he rarely travelled beyond the borders of Scotland and then only briefly. In a geographical and personal sense Maclean's whole experience was provincial, but this limitation did not blunt his belief in Internationalism rather it may have served to create an idealised version which survived the shock of war. In any event the Maclean of this early period was a fairly conventional if energetic social democrat, a generally loyal provincial supporter of Hyndman. Such a reputation as he enjoyed was based on his role as Marxist teacher and it spread only slowly beyond Glasgow and Scotland.

In the immediate aftermath of the 1906 general election Maclean continued, as before, to devote most of his spare time from school-teaching promoting the SDF's cause through street-corner propaganda, Marxist education classes and his activities in the co-operative movement. His intense commitment to the Marxist cause was already recognised and continued to be so even after his marriage to Agnes Wood in 1909 and the birth of two daughters in quick succession. This change in his domestic circumstances does not seem to have interrupted substantially the course or pace of Maclean's political activity; the dynamic pattern had already been set.

In the summer months of July and August 1906 Maclean once more embarked on his traditional, exhausting speaking tour of Scotland, but the political highlight of his year was the creation of an SDF branch in his home-town of Pollokshaws in October.[2] This branch was created almost single-handedly, following a series of open-air meetings held in the locality.[3] Maclean attracted a small but enthusiastic core of adherents who ensured that the branch maintained a lively, vital presence in Pollokshaws and its environs up to the war. He supplied much of the necessary optimism and zeal, training a number of members in the art of public speaking, holding public meetings and encouraging the branch to contest elections to local representative bodies. A limited success was achieved with the election to the Eastwood School Board of two members, Robert Blair and James Mac-Dougall, by 1914.[4]

It was through the Pollokshaws Branch that Maclean was to forge the most fruitful political relationship of his career with James MacDougall, the branch's sixteen-year-old inaugural secretary. MacDougall was the son of a prominent local Liberal politician and the nephew of one of Maclean's erstwhile colleagues in the Progressive Union. Employed originally as a clerk with the Clydesdale Bank, from which he was dismissed on account of his political activities, MacDougall was to become Maclean's political protégé and then his closest political colleague and associate almost until the end of the latter's life.

Like Maclean, MacDougall became an active member of the co-operative movement and but for his anti-war stance might have achieved real prominence in that movement. Had he chosen the more orthodox political route for aspiring socialists offered by the ILP rather than the more difficult path of Maclean and social democracy, MacDougall's intellectual gifts, outstanding ability as a public speaker and pleasant personal manner could have opened up the real possibility of office in a Labour government. As it was MacDougall was destined to tread a path that would lead to imprisonment, consequential ill-health and poverty, and to a nomadic political life which saw him in the CPGB, the Liberal Party, the New Party, though not the Fascist Party, before ending his days as a kind of maverick Conservative anti-Catholic.[5]

In the following year, 1908, Maclean established another important political relationship with a Russian political emigré, Peter Petroff.[6] Born in Novotorzhsk in 1884, the youngest of a family of nine, Petroff became an apprentice cabinet-maker and attended the University of Kiev as a substitute for an idle student. He joined the Russian Social Democratic Labour Party (SDLP) in 1901 and participated in an insurrection in Voronezh as part of the 1905 Revolution, after which he was captured and imprisoned. Petroff subsequently escaped from captivity and eventually made his way to Britain in search of his older brother Michael Beck, a cabinet-maker in London.

Petroff came first to the port of Leith near Edinburgh in a destitute state and was directed to Maclean in Glasgow, with whom he stayed for almost two months, learning and perfecting his knowledge of English. Thereafter Petroff made his way to London, where he became an active member of the Kentish Town Branch of the SDP and a participant in the foundation of the London Labour Party. Unlike many of the Russian emigré colony in London Petroff's commitment to the SDP was more than token, and he rapidly assumed a prominent position on its left wing. Willie Gallacher was later to ascribe particular influence over Maclean to Petroff.[7] H. Lee, Secretary to the SDP and later editor of *Justice*, was to blame the influence of Russian emigrés, without specifically mentioning Petroff, for Maclean's subsequent break with Hyndman and the 'old guard' of social democracy.[8]

However, there is little evidence that the two maintained very close contact before 1914 and less to suggest that Maclean was influenced at all by Petroff at this time. There is in fact little to suggest that Maclean's political views changed much between 1906, and 1914 as a result of any influence exerted by Petroff. Such change as did occur can be located in Maclean's basic conception of social democracy.

One important influence on Maclean at this time was his involvement in the dramatic events surrounding the 1907 Belfast Dock Strike which united, for a brief moment, elements of the Catholic and Protestant labouring classes in Belfast. Maclean arrived in Belfast while on his annual exhausting summer propaganda tour of Scotland and northern England. Between 21 and 28 July he had been in the Cowdenbeath area where he addressed twenty-one meetings speaking as many as five times a day, later moving on to Belfast for the weekend of 1-3 August before moving back to England and Carlisle and South Shields by 7 August.[9] Such an undertaking was tiring enough, but the experience in Belfast clearly exhilarated Maclean.

He had been invited over, along with Victor Grayson, the recent socialist victor at the Colne Valley by-election, by the strike leader James Larkin.[10] Maclean found the situation electrifying and full of implications for his conception of the process of social transformation. He spoke before enthusiastic mass meetings of a size he could hardly have encountered before: 'Addressed strikers at night. Audience of thousands. Labourers mad to join trade unions. All Irish towns the same. Had three monster meetings ... about 10,000 present, some estimated 15,000. Had a meeting of 1,000 on Monday night.'[11]

Maclean left Belfast before the strike ended and before the military were involved in an 'exchange' with 'rioters' which left three civilians dead. These events were redolent, in the minds of socialists, with the Featherstone shootings during the coal dispute of 1893 when the use of military force, with a Liberal government in power, left a number dead. This connection was emphasised in the person of Herbert Asquith, a member of both the 1893 and the contemporary Liberal government. Much criticism was poured on Augustine Birrell, the Irish Secretary, for not taking measures to initiate arbitration in a dispute and general situation which was obviously tense and potentially explosive.

Maclean wrote in such terms in his account of the Belfast events for *Justice*.[12] The argument drew the rejoinder from the ILP'er, Philip Snowden, that such criticisms were written by fools who failed to recognise the culpable role played by inflammatory demagogues in the dispute.[18] Maclean immediately responded in the columns of the *Scottish Co-operator*, again blaming Birrell for his political inertia and asserting that Snowden ought not to absolve individuals from responsibility and lay the blame on social structures without drawing the necessary conclusion: 'If we hold the capitalists to blame, let us remove them from power: if we hold that not they, but the social structure is to blame, again let us remove them from power so as to change the social structure.' For Maclean the events in Belfast demonstrated the underlying reality of the class war which could only be answered effectively along social democratic lines: 'Class society requires class politics, a class press, class organisations.'[14]

Maclean's belief that the Belfast strike pointed a way forward for Irish workers divided on religious lines proved illusory, but his view on trade union activism was undoubtedly altered. Before this experience Maclean's only direct contact with trade unionism derived from his observations of the situation on Clydeside, where trade unionism was narrowly centred on a relatively highly-skilled, exclusive group of workers who reflected the kinds of attitudes associated with the idea of a labour aristocracy. Such observations as Maclean made confirmed a general pessimism as to the value of trade unions as a vehicle for social change and led him to emphasise the limitations of trade union activity. Now he had witnessed, at first hand, the radicalising effects of a major industrial struggle on a large body of unskilled workers and this was reflected in a more positive attitude to trade union organisation. In 1909 he urged the need to organise unskilled labourers in Scotland and observed: 'Despite all the pessimism of disappointed trade unionists, I feel convinced that trade organisation is a requisite of socialist organisation, since it enables the workers to wage the class conflict on a higher plane and prepares the way for the higher Socialist organisation.'[15]

But Maclean remained careful to distinguish support for strikes as a means of raising consciousness from a belief in the syndicalist idea of industrial struggle as the mechanism of social transformation. Syndicalism was illegitimate as far as Maclean was concerned because it was overtly sectional in character and failed to recognise the primacy of political action. He would have agreed with Hyndman that 'strikes, syndicalism, anarchy are but varying forms of restless working-class ignorance, or despairing revolts against undeniable oppression'.[16] But he would no longer accept the view that strikes could do nothing to 'emancipate the propertyless class'. While holding fast to the social democratic belief in the central importance of politics Maclean now made more space in his Marxism to accommodate the reality of industrial militancy than most of his social democratic contemporaries.[17] This left him better prepared to react to the wave of labour miltancy after 1911 and to recognise its revolutionary potential during and immediately after the war.

The growth of industrial conflict in the years after 1907 undoubtedly forced itself on to the agenda of both capitalists and socialists. However, a more immediate preoccupation for social democrats concerned the appropriate role to be adopted in relation to the Labour Party. A growing body of social democratic opinion began to voice doubts over their continued estrangement from the Labour Party, which followed the decision to disaffiliate from the LRC in 1901. The results of the 1906 general election stimulated the debate further since the rapid improvement in Labour's Parliamentary representation contrasted starkly with the disastrous performance of the SDF. In such an atmosphere the question of reaffiliation resurfaced.

Opponents, notably Harry Quelch and Theodore Rothstein, argued that the change of name from LRC to Labour Party in 1906 could not obscure the fact that it was still the creature of the trade unions and remained ultimately an anti-socialist body. It was, they argued, an illusion to believe that the re-entry of the social democrats would make Labour socialist: rather, to the contrary, social democracy would become diluted.[18] For Quelch, the most important anti-affiliationist, the correct strategy was to remain outside the Labour Party and trust that a growing body of ILP'ers would come to see the sterile consequences of their association with the existing Labour Alliance for the spread of socialism.[19] Once this 'reality' was recognised it would be possible to look for 'socialist unity' between the ILP and social democracy. This had been thwarted by ILP leaders at the end of the 1890s, but still remained the goal of many like Quelch.

Maclean was in favour of reaffiliation because he believed that the Labour Party was fundamentally different from the old LRC. He had viewed that body as the expression of narrowly conceived trade union interests, hostile to socialism in either its Marxist or ILP forms: 'Richard Bell, to safeguard his Union and himself after the Taff Vale decision, gave the lead to the formation of the L.R.C which undoubtedly came into being to protect trade unions, their funds and the salaries of paid officials.'[20]

Despite this vision of trade union cynicism Maclean recognised that most socialists viewed the LRC as the starting-point from which could emerge a genuine, workers' party that would be impelled, inevitably, towards the socialist objective of capturing economic power. He accepted the logical consequence that the SDF had been premature in trying to force a socialist objective on the LRC so early in its existence, and wrong to withdraw when that objective had been rejected.[21] After 1906, Maclean, like Hyndman, saw the return of the thirty Labour MPs as 'marvellous' and the change from LRC to Labour Party in a positive light: 'It did not matter to me how some had won. A new party now existed to champion the cause of Labour.'[22]

This belief rested, not only on the results of an election or a change of name, but a change of attitude on the part of Labour The socialist element seemed more confident and assertive, while the 'Liberal' trade union wing appeared to be in eclipse. There were also encouraging signs in the growing contacts between Labour MPs and social democrats in the campaign for a Right To Work Bill in 1907-08 and, more generally, on the whole issue of the unemployed. Labourites such as Hardie, Seddon, Roberts and O'Grady worked closely and openly with Hyndman, Quelch and other social democrats, most importantly in London where the social democrats often took the initiative and held key posts in the various campaign agencies.[23]

These developing relationships, taken together with the spectacular by-election victories won by Grayson standing as an Independent socialist in Colne Valley and Peter Curran fighting as a 'socialist' Labour Party candidate in Jarrow, created an impression that a socialist tide was swelling, both outside and inside the Labour Party. It was noticeable that socialist resolutions were more often debated and endorsed at Labour Conferences after 1906 than before.[24] Maclean was obviously impressed by the Amalgamated Society of Engineers' resolution, framed boldly in support of the common ownership principle, and submitted to the 1907 Labour Party conference. While Philip Snowden correctly cautioned that such a resolution, even if passed, would amount only to an 'expression of opinion' and not a definite commitment, Maclean took a decidedly optimistic view. He argued that the ASE resolution was so unequivocally socialist that its passage at the conference could not be understated. It would mean 'that the Party should avow itself a revolutionary socialist party and come out from under the transparent cloak of a vague, indefinite, purposeless, so-called Labourism ... not fear, but persistent propaganda will win the day. We want a few more Blatchfords, Hyndmans, Quelches and Graysons and the people are ours'.[25]

In April 1908, *Justice* reported that the Pollokshaws' SDP Branch unanimously favoured reaffiliation to the Labour Party.[26] In the same month Maclean proclaimed 'the Labour Party is hopelessly socialist now despite the presence of non-socialists at present within its Parliamentary ranks, ... If we join the Labour Party then the enemy will shout more vehemently than ever that the Labour Party is a socialist party and it will not take long to make it so.'[27] Maclean still took this position as late as January 1909 when he argued that liberalism was losing its grip on Labour, while the socialist influence continued to grow: 'Who urged the formation of the L.R.C? Richard Bell. Who today wishes to kill the Labour Party? Richard Bell. Why? Because the socialists have defeated his purpose of binding the Labour Party to the Liberals, or, at least, made it impossible for him to sit on the Liberal benches.'[28]

Yet Maclean's attitude rapidly gave way to a gloomier assessment. Like Hyndman he came to see Liberalism as maintaining and even strengthening its hold over Labour politicians whose attitude to social democrats was one of increasing hostility. 'The Labour MP's have fawned upon Asquith and his crew whilst ... using the vilest language against Grayson, Blatchford, Hyndman and others ... Whatever is proposed by the SDP is misrepresented, caricatured or opposed; but whatever comes from the Liberals receives adulation.'[29] He even rejected the idea that

Labour was a genuinely independent political force, denouncing the conduct of those Labour MPs who 'silently listen to a wearisome discussion of the Licensing Bill during a period of almost unparallelled unemployment and starvation for the workers, and who strut about on liberal temperance platforms, exhorting the starving to end their drunken habits'.[30]

Such independent action as Labour was capable of mounting occurred only when its own specific interests were at stake, as in the case of the Osborne Judgement which rendered the use of trade union funds for political purposes illegal and thereby threatened the whole financial basis of the Labour Party. Maclean contrasted the intense level of Labour Party activity on this issue with their immobilism when it came to supporting Belfast and Tyneside strikers or Grayson's protests against the treatment of the unemployed. Thus activity was justified in protest against the 'awful decision' in the Osborne case 'that will deprive them of their wages' but rejected in the other cases as 'not statesmanlike'.[31]

This picture of an ineffective Labour Party trapped in the Liberal political embrace was widely held within the Labour Alliance and especially within the ILP. Perhaps the best known articulator of this view was Victor Grayson who not only challenged the Labour Party with his brand of Parliamentary pyrotechnics but criticised the ILP leaders Hardie, MacDonald, Glasier and Snowden for their failure to put the socialist case with conviction. By the occasion of the ILP Annual Conference of 1909 Grayson's criticisms of the party's 'old guard' had provoked an internal crisis and he was seen by his opponents as a subversive force seeking to create a split within the Party.[32]

There was open talk of the possibility of creating a 'new' fighting socialist party out of dissident elements of the ILP, taking their cue from Grayson and the SDP as well as Blatchford's Clarion groups and various local socialist clubs and organisations.[33] Certainly by 1909-10 the movement for affiliation to the Labour Party within the SDP gave way, temporarily at least, to enthusiasm for the experiment of a realignment of socialist forces outside the Labour Party, and the hope that such a realignment would provide a platform for the development of socialism as a mass popular movement.

While Maclean was involved in the continuing speculation about a realignment of socialist organisations outside the Labour Party he continued to play an active role within the co-operative movement in Scotland. Indeed the co-operatives remained an important platform for Maclean in his attempt to spread the social democratic message to a mass audience and, more narrowly, in his attempt to compete with the increasingly influential ILP in the struggle to push the co-operatives in a socialist direction. Together with James MacDougall, Maclean attended co-operative meetings assiduously and used the co-operative press to raise issues and promote socialist arguments. The close interconnection between Maclean's role as a social democrat and a co-operator is reflected in the fact that his first pamphlet published by the Social Democrats entitled 'The Greenock Jungle', a study in the sale of adulterated meat by Greenock butchers, was clearly inspired by the current preoccupations of local co-operative societies.[34]

Throughout his association with the co-operatives, Maclean addressed issues of a 'bread and butter' kind and assisted in the provision of courses designed to improve the ability of the members to speak in public. But ultimately Maclean's preoccupation was with the dissemination of Marxist ideas and his intervention via the letters pages of the *Scottish Co-operator* was generally to that end. On occasion Maclean contributed to an exchange of letters enlightening in terms of what issues were important at particular times and illuminating in terms of what they reveal about his ideas and approach.

During 1908, Maclean was involved in a fairly heated exchange of letters concerned with the contemporary relevance of Marx's theory of value and later involving the relationship between religion and social progress.[35] The debate was initiated by a letter attacking Marx's theory of value as worthless, citing the work of the Austrian economist Bohm-Bawerk in support of the contention. Bohm-Bawerk had published a critique of Marx in 1896 which was re-published in Britain two years later as 'Karl Marx and the Close of his System'. Stuart Macintyre has stated that Bohm-Bawerk's thesis, based on the contention that there was a contradiction within Marx's theory of value as outlined in elaborate detail in Volume I of *Capital* but apparently abandoned in Volume III, provided important ammunition in the arsenal of anti-Marxist polemics.[36]

The Bohm-Bawerk thesis was one which British Marxists had great difficulty refuting with any degree of confidence and conviction, even when English translations of Marxist defences by Hilferding (1919) and Bukharin (1927) became available. In the pre-1914 period British Marxists were dependent on their own ability to interpret *Capital* or on the explanation offered by one of the leading social democrats. Interestingly, Henry Hyndman himself wrote a series of articles on the subject in *Justice* during October and November 1907 designed to equip Marxists with a defence to an argument which must have been faced increasingly often.[37]

In practice however, if Macintyre is right, most Marxists responded to criticism by simply restating Marx's theory as firmly as possible while trenchantly denouncing the critics. This certainly seems to have characterised Maclean's approach in the *Scottish Co-operator* and a little later in the Glasgow ILP's *Forward* newspaper. There is little evidence of an intellectually credible riposte from Maclean, and his opponents, ILP–Fabians of a sophisticated kind, remained unimpressed. Maclean's counter-arguments are rather those of someone satisfied to attack the critics rather than address the criticism, and to refer them back to Marx whose 'writings are today more powerful than ever before'.[38]

In some respects such an approach was inevitable, given the nature of a propagandist exchange in a relatively 'popular' newspaper where the amount of space was in any event restricted. Certainly Maclean saw himself as 'defending' his political side and expressed surprise when a contributor observed that he was completely unyielding in his views. Nevertheless Maclean's arguments on surplus value are weak and unconvincing and this may point up what some have seen as his lack of originality in interpreting Marx. His strength as a Marxist teacher of economics lay in his ability to convey key Marxist concepts to audiences of working men, often with little formal education beyond a basic level, in a way which connected with their everyday experience. Thus his students were instructed in the complexity of company balance sheets and the general issues of contemporary political economy as interpreted through a Marxist lens.

Some critics of Maclean, notably SLP'ers, pointed out that his teaching was purely a matter of simple propaganda and that his classes did not produce the crop of Marxist teachers which the SLP generated.[39] Orthodox economics teachers might acknowledge that Maclean could attract an audience to his classes but complained that Marxist economics teaching was simply propaganda if not accompanied by the study of classic economic theory. Maclean clearly believed that only Marxist economics held any real relevance to working men but he was not oblivious to contemporary economic debates and saw himself as a serious, political economist alive to the changing nature of economic and technological development. Thus he was quickly aware of the likely impact of new technological and managerial techniques on working practices which allowed Clydeside shipyards 'to turn out larger vessels with fewer hands in a shorter time than ever before . . . What applies to shipbuilding applies to railways, wheat, cotton and even expensive luxuries such as motor cars.'[40]

He was also interested in the problem of explaining price rises and in particular how they connected with the production of gold and, much later, the expansion of paper money. The monetarist approach which I. S. McLean correctly observed in the post-war pamphlet 'Burn Bradbury' was not as he suggests, an odd abberation, but a consistent feature of John Maclean's explanation of price rises.

Whatever Maclean's deficiences might have been as an economic theorist it is clear that his classes proved attractive to a growing audience of working-class men. One testament to Maclean's appeal is provided by a very senior police officer called upon to investigate the nature of these classes during the war. He reported that they had attracted 'thousands', mainly of the artisan class, who appeared satisfied with the experience. Moreover, any money generated had gone into payment for the hire of halls and to cover other expenses. Maclean had not bene-fited in any personal financial sense from his activities.[41]

The appeal of such classes encouraged Maclean's belief in the need to increase the availability of Marxist-based classes and, ideally, to set up a Scottish Labour College. This objective now became central to his activity and he tried to develop support for it within the wider Scottish labour movement. To this end he welcomed what he saw as the growing willingness of the Scottish co-operative movement to support his teaching approach. He informed interested readers that he had

> so far interested educationalists in co-operative circles that next winter they will spend more of their money in running economic and industrial history classes with Marxists as their teachers, because Marxism . . . affords the best training for those who hope to guide such a vast and complex undertaking as the co-operative production and distribution of commodities.[42]

Again and again Maclean and MacDougall were to push their case for more Marxist-based education at co-operative meetings and conferences before the war; from the local and regional levels right up to the Co-operative Congress itself.

On the relationship between religion and social progress Maclean saw no merit in the argument that religion had acted as a force for progress. For him Christianity had left Scotland seething with social sores after nineteen centuries and, rather than a source of progress, represented an obstacle to social advance and the possibility of building a society based on human brotherhood. It was, therefore, not a 'means by which we may banish pain and sorrow from society'.[43] The downfall of capitalism and its associated evils could only be achieved by the pursuit of socialism via the class struggle, an activity which was itself morally uplifting 'from the philosophic point of view'.[44] To that end Maclean continued to urge those interested to read 'the writings of Hyndman, Bax, Quelch and Blatchford . . . [where] . . . he will find the workers' position more accurately portrayed, capitalism more thoroughly examined and reform proposals more efficient for the stopping of the robbery of today'.[45]

Up to this point, about 1910, there is little in Maclean's public statements to suggest his political line is other than consistent with the position of the social democratic 'old guard' and especially Hyndman and Quelch, with whom he maintained good personal relations. Maclean's initial support for reaffiliation to the Labour Party and subsequent disillusion with such a move mirrored closely Hyndman's attitude. On the problem of Marx's theory of value his intervention in a debate in the *Scottish Co-operator* again broadly followed the arguments outlined by Hyndman in *Justice*. This is not to say that Maclean was a mere cipher for Hyndman or Quelch but to underline the fact that he was very much a Marxist in the orthodox social democratic mould who energetically supported in Scotland the broad policy and agitational positions of social democracy.

Perhaps the most interesting example of this in the light of subsequent events was Maclean's support for the policy of the Citizen Army. In 1908 he moved a resolution to the Scottish Conference of the SDP: 'That in view of the possibility of an attack on Britain by the German Empire we demand that all citizens be trained in the use of arms and each have a rifle and ammunition ready for use at a moment's notice.'[46] This resolution is directly derived from Hyndman and while it can be seen as a tactical manoeuvre to counter the setting up of a Territorial Army by the Establishment and as a ploy by the SDP to forestall the possibility of conscription, it is significant that Maclean accepts the possibility of a German invasion and the consequent need to resist such an invasion. This kind of 'defencist' position was used by social democrats on the outbreak of war as a means of resolving the difficult choice between supporting or opposing the war. By then it was no longer a policy Maclean was prepared to endorse.

On a more mundane level Maclean followed Hyndman's lead in attacking Temperance Reformers for maintaining a politically distracting and 'scientifically' wrong-headed view on the cause of working-class poverty and general distress. Using the letters columns of the *Scottish Co-operator* to challenge the Temperance case put forward by the anti-drinks campaigner, David Scrimgeour, Maclean argued that the trade in alcholic drink was only a small fraction of British capitalism's activity, a 'bagatelle compared with the amount taken from Labour as surplus value'. Its abolition would not materially affect the general position of the working classes. Nonetheless, he urged Scrimgeour to join 'our party', which shows instances of marvellous influence over the drinking habits of the workers. He pointed specifically to the recent Congress of 'our' German party which urged workers to abstain from spirits, and the example of Sweden, where the socialist leaders of the trade unions persuaded the bulk of their members to abstain from drink during the recent general strike. That advice had led, in turn, to a recent vote in favour of prohibition.[47]

In another instance, Maclean led the protest to the Spanish Consulate in Glasgow following the execution of Francisco Ferrer, a Catalan anarchist and progressive educationalist.[48] The Ferrer case assumed the status of the Spanish 'Dreyfus' incident, with Ferrer seen as the victim of a judicial murder instigated by religious and reactionary forces on account of his political views and reputation as a 'free-thinker'. The Glasgow demonstration was a relatively small affair but it was part of a series of protests throughout Britain and supported the much more impressive protest mounted by Hyndman and the SDP in London. It was another example of Maclean's energy in organising action in line with national SDP policy.[49]

Although Maclean has often been represented as an intransigent sectarian in politics he was always willing to support and work alongside other socialists, notably ILP'ers, while remaining sceptical about their motives. One area where a common campaign was mounted was on the plight of the unemployed. Maclean had been involved in attempts at organising the Glasgow unemployed as early as 1905. After 1908 the employment position in Glasgow deteriorated sharply and it was reported that the local unemployment situation in the Winter of 1908-09 was the worst since 1862.[50] Maclean was involved in attempts to highlight the plight of the unemployed, involving a celebrated incident when Prince Arthur was 'hooted' during a 'demi-semi-royal visit' to Glasgow in 1908.[51]

In 1909, following the publication of the Minority Report of the Poor Law Commission and in line with SDP policy, Maclean was at the forefront of attempts to win support for the setting up of farm colonies as a means of ameliorating unemployment.

Although the SDP favoured the development of a nationally organised and regulated scheme, Maclean worked on a locally based Umemployed Workers Committee, trying to persuade Renfrewshire County Council to initiate a farm colony. He addressed the Quarterly meeting of the Renfrewshire Co-operative Association which agreed a resolution supporting the idea 'as a means of mitigating unemployment'.[52]

While there were plenty of issues on which a broad front of ILP and social democratic rank-and-filers could be brought together on Clydeside, it was not an alliance of equals. Although the SDP had grown from the rock-bottom position occupied by the SDF in 1903, it was increasingly overshadowed by the ILP, aided by the Glasgow *Forward* newspaper, with its mixture of left-wing politics and electoral pragmatism. Both were in turn marginal actors in a region still overwhelmingly Liberal in political sentiment.

Maclean saw himself as almost personally responsible for maintaining the credibility of the SDP as an independent political force on Clydeside and to that end defended the Party's record against all comers. When the editor of the *Scottish Co-operator* ridiculed the social democrats as politically irrelevant and unwilling to listen and learn, Maclean indignantly upbraided him, pointing to the growing influence of Marxist education classes and the activities of locally elected SDP'ers like George Hale in Govan as examples of the Party's significance.[53] Again when Thomas Johnston, editor of *Forward*, claimed the Marxist mantle for the ILP, Maclean engaged him in a series of exchanges in the paper's columns, rejecting the validity of Johnston's claim and asserting the primacy of the SDP as the authentic voice of Marxism.[54] And yet Maclean could scarcely ignore the underlying fragility of the SDP on Clydeside and, indeed, in Scotland.

The two general elections of 1910 confirmed the Liberal Party's domination of Clydeside politics and emphasised the general weakness of the Labour Party in Scotland. The SDP was reduced to the role of mere spectator, fighting only one Scottish constituency. Maclean reacted to the situation, departing from the SDP's policy of advocating abstention by working-class electors when confronted by a straight Liberal–Unionist contest, by urging, instead, a vote for the Unionists.[55] He justified this advice by the need to challenge the prevailing tendency to see the Liberals as in some way preferable to the Unionists, when both were committed, in fact, to capitalism. Such a view seemed eccentric as a practical mechanism for winning workers to Marxism and may have reflected his growing frustration at the SDP's failure to count politically. Certainly, the prospects for socialism of an SDP variety on Clydeside seemed dim perhaps desperately so. As a leading Scottish ILP'er put it shortly after the elections: 'If anyone thinks that Scotland is to be won to what is vaguely called 'Revolutionary Socialism', then I am afraid that person is in for a disappointment.'[56] For Maclean, despite the frustrations and obstacles to social democratic advance, these were still days of hope and while the days of disappointment approached, they were some way off.

3 A Left opposition

For social democrats the years after 1910 were marked by a mixture of frustration, disappointment and factional disputes, culminating in the calamity of the war which finally shattered the whole edifice of social democracy. Initial disappointment surrounded the performance of the SDP at the general elections of 1910 where the meagre popular vote secured by its candidates showed how little had been the advance on the poor position achieved by the SDF four years previously. Certainly social democracy seemed as far away as ever from building a mass working-class base which had always been its objective. Further disappointment attended the creation of the British Social Party (BSP) in 1911.

This body formed as a result of the merger between the SDP, dissident ILP branches, Clarion and local socialist clubs represented the fruits of the campaign for the realignment of the Left which had been canvassed with increasing enthusiasm in 1909 and 1910.[1] In reality the BSP was little more than an extension of the SDP to include an assorted fraction of those socialists disillusioned by the performance of the Labour Party. But as long as the overwhelming bulk of the ILP remained committed to the alliance with the trade unions in the Labour Party the realignment of the socialist Left remained little more than an aspiration.

If the experience of the SDP/BSP provided social democrats with small scope for confidence in the future they could at least call on their reserves of Marxist faith and belief in the international strength of their movement to sustain them. A more telling blow against the cohesion of British social democracy in the longer term came from an unexpected quarter. Towards the end of 1910 Henry Hyndman publicly endorsed a policy urging a massive increase in government expenditure on the Royal Navy as a response to the perceived threat to Britain posed by Germany's programme of building warships.[2] Such a policy had been the subject of much discussion among Liberal and Conservative politicians and in the editorials of national newspapers. But for Britain's leading Marxist to endorse such an expenditure came as a blow to those social democrats who saw it as a betrayal of the fundamental belief in international working-class brotherhood and as standing in direct contradiction to the position of the Socialist International.[3]

In retrospect Hyndman's commitment to the so-called 'Big Navy' set social democrats on the path of increasingly bitter division which was finally resolved by the split in their ranks which took place in 1915. This split effectively destroyed social democracy. It is perhaps worth noting that Hyndman's analysis of international events and support for a strong policy of national defence was quite widely shared within the social democratic camp and among some of the leading socialists, like Robert Blatchford and Victor Grayson. Nor was this debate unique to the small British social democratic party; there were similar divisions of view on defence issues in all the main European socialist parties.

It is unhelpful to characterise the Hyndmanite policy as an exercise in rabid jingoism. This may be acceptable at a polemical level but it does not assist us in understanding why Hyndman's declaration could not be dismissed as idiosyncratic. If it had been an outburst of simple jingoism it is doubtful that social democrats would have taken it as seriously as they obviously did, or that it would have divided them so deeply. Certainly Hyndman, Quelch and Lee believed that their position reflected a more realistic evaluation of the international situation and the real strength of international social democracy than that put forward by their opponents.

As this debate unfolded Maclean continued to work energetically for the social democratic cause, and responded to the issues raised by Hyndman in a surprisingly restrained manner. We say surprisingly because it is generally assumed, and often asserted, that Maclean emerged as one of the leading actors in the anti-Hyndman campaign. This would seem a reasonable assumption given Maclean's oft-stated commitment to the principle of International Brotherhood and his subsequent suffering for that cause during the war. Yet for most of the time between 1910 and 1914 he did not play a prominent role in the struggle against the social patriots. He was certainly not involved directly in the battles at the highest levels of the BSP until 1913 at the earliest. This is not to say that he was confused by the issue since his position was clear and unchanged. He was committed to the Internationalist position in an unwavering fashion. Once Hyndman made his position public in *The Morning Post*, arguing for an increase in naval expenditure by an additional sum of £100 million,[4] the Pollokshaws' Branch was quick to react: 'this branch recognises the international solidarity of the working-class and therefore deprecates Comrade Hyndman's agitation for a big navy as tending rather to break down than to build up the essential unity of the workers of the world'.[5]

But while framed in impeccable social democratic terms the use of words like *deprecates* and *as tending to* might be thought to soften the thrust of the resolution. The tone is not as uncompromising or sharp as Maclean's later contributions to polemical debate. More significant than this semantic analysis of a resolution was something Maclean wrote in an article published by *Justice* on another subject. Maclean raised the naval question, in passing, attributing Hyndman's intervention to his 'super anxiety' about the perceived German war menace and stating: 'I am one of those who believe that Hyndman's warning, *needful though it might have been,* has partially led to distraction from the real object we have in view, the emancipation of all wage slaves from capitalist robbery.'[6]

The implication of this statement was that Maclean recognised that there might be some cause for anxiety about Germany's intentions but believed Hyndman's reaction was extreme. Moreover the effect of Hyndman's policy was bound to damage the social democratic cause. It was damaging in principle because it opened them up to the charge that they were not true Internationalists, and this was levelled at them by the ILP. It was more damaging in the sense that it necessarily divided the party and diverted its energies away from the revolutionary objective and towards internal dissent. Maclean's criticism of Hyndman, then, was made at two levels. On the one hand he opposed the substance of Hyndman's policy as contrary to social democratic principle and made this clear enough in public. But the main emphasis of his opposition was directed at the consequences for social democracy of pursuing a line which Maclean saw as an unnecessary distraction.

The question then emerges: why should Maclean have emphasised the practical consequences of Hyndman's policy rather than its implications in terms of fundamental principle? The answer seems to lie in the depth of his faith in the strength and principled character of International Social Democracy. As we have seen, Hyndman justified his stand in terms of political realism as to the warlike intentions of the German State dominated by the 'Junker Class'. He interpreted its military, and especially its naval growth as a clear manifestation of its aggressive character. Hyndman also believed that neither the Socialist International, as a collective entity, nor Germany's social democracy were capable of constraining the German State. Indeed he cited unnamed, senior German socialists in support of this pessimistic assessment of the capacity of the German SDP to stop an aggressive war.[7] Given this assessment of the situation, the Hyndmanites were virtually bound to support a policy of building up Britain's naval strength to meet such a threat.

Maclean, by contrast, clearly clung firmly to the view that the anti-war position of the Socialist International, solemnly affirmed by its constituent parties in various resolutions before 1914, would be effective. He, like, Lenin and even Keir Hardie, expected the anti-war position to be implemented successfully in the event of belligerent activity on the part of any of the Great Powers. Moreover, he held it was the duty of each 'national' socialist party to ensure that the commitment to Internationalism was carried out in practice. A move by Hyndman to improve the naval capacity of Britain was not compatible with such a commitment. Moreover, Hyndman's policy was an unnecessary distraction since, even if the German Junkers were bent on war, Maclean was confident they would be blocked by German social democrats.

The difference between Hyndman and Maclean on this issue turned not on the question of Germany's intentions but their contrasting estimation of the power of international social democracy to combine against such intentions. But it is nonetheless interesting that Maclean did not confront Hyndman head-on. After all he was in no doubt as to the potential damage that Hyndman's declaration could and would inflict on the social democratic camp. It is possible that he viewed Hyndman's position as an abberation which would cease to be relevant after the initial controversy died down. It is certainly the case that as the defence issue rumbled on and came to involve wider questions like the control of the Party newspaper *Justice*, Maclean became more actively engaged in the Party conflict at a higher level. Before 1913 he seems to have been satisfied to simply affirm his commitment to Internationalism, point out the error of Hyndman's policy and judgement, and continue to pursue his individual political initiatives.

Such an approach may offer important clues as to how Maclean viewed the nature of the socialist party and the role and responsibilities of its members. In fact the social democratic party had always been relatively relaxed in its approach to discipline, being a loose association of individuals bound together by a shared political faith rather than a tightly knit centrally organised group. For Maclean personal integrity was a substitute for an externally imposed discipline, and in times of crisis he tended to respond by going his own way politically without either fighting for his position in the Party or leaving it. Neither now nor in 1915 nor 1920, did he pursue his opposition on an important point of policy or principle to the point of splitting the Party in the way of a Lenin. Indeed Maclean's implicit criticism of Hyndman was that he was risking such a split by his policy of naval rearmament. This seems to have been a risk Maclean wished to avoid if at all possible. Instead he reacted in a highly individualistic and autonomous fashion.

As Kendall observes, Maclean's role in the internal struggles of the BSP before the war was rather limited, characterised more by silence than the strident articulation of political principle.[8] Indeed at about the time that the struggle between Hyndmanites and anti-Hyndmanites began to reach a climax Maclean accepted an offer from Hyndman to contribute 'Scottish Notes' to *Justice*.[9] This he did under the pseudonym 'Gael'. From 1911 to the war his contributions to *Justice* concentrated specifically on Scottish developments and contained little to suggest the sharp ideological struggle currently taking place within the BSP. Certainly the Hyndmanites spoke of Maclean in respectful terms in the years down to the war. In practice Maclean's preoccupations over these years were focused fairly narrowly on a range of issues which again reflected his Scottish location and perspective. His energies were poured into campaigns such as those designed to create a Scottish Labour College, to persuade the Scottish co-operatives to adopt a definite socialist line in politics, or at least to develop formal political links with the wider labour and trade union movement and to develop a housing policy capable of tackling the appalling housing conditions of the Clydeside working class.

While never reflecting a nationalist perspective Maclean's political stage remained, as before, firmly rooted in Scotland and the experience of the working class of the Clyde region. But despite this restricted regional base of activity it needs to be emphasised that Maclean saw his role in the wider context of International Socialism, and he and MacDougall lost no opportunity to express their faith in the Internationalist ideal. That commitment was so deeply rooted that their reaction to the war when it came was unhesitatingly expressed in terms of their Internationalist faith.

But the most significant development in Maclean's political practice at this time, which held important consequences for his subsequent approach, concerned the rising tide of industrial militancy. As we have argued previously, Maclean's views on the political significance of industrial struggle had been modified by his experience of the 1907 Belfast Dock Strike. The orthodox social democrat approach to strikes emphasised their defensive character and political limitations. They constituted, in short, a working-class reflex action in the face of capitalist power, ultimately devoid of political possibilities. Maclean had come to a more positive assessment of the role which industrial militancy could play in the emergence of a revolutionary consciousness amongst workers. Strikes were important in that they revealed the 'true' nature of the capitalist system to workers and provided illustrations of 'the real class war that are more effective than all the theory we might fire at our benighted class from this 'till doomsday. Fighting leads to new facts, thus to our new theory and thence to revolution.'[10]

While Scotland was not at the centre of this growing cycle of industrial militancy and unrest it was nonetheless affected by it. The generally calm industrial relations situation which had frustrated industrial and political agitators like Maclean began to change. Nor were the growing number of industrial disputes restricted to the traditional sectors of coal mining, engineering or the docks. Now in a period of high employment and rapidly changing methods of production, groups of workers not noted for their militancy, nor even for being unionised, became involved in disputes. Women and unskilled men reacted against the imposition of production methods associated with an extreme form of the division of labour and payments by results.

The actual causes of disputes might vary from one situation to another but they tended to involve questions of the piece rate, alienation from the work process itself and a reaction against modern managerial techniques. Two such disputes which concerned Maclean at this time were the Neilston thread mills dispute and the more famous strike at the Singer Sewing Machine plant on Clydebank. In the case of the Neilston strike Maclean was actively involved in its organisation while in the Singer dispute he chronicled and analysed the events for *Justice*. Both were part of the increasing number of Scottish disputes which led Maclean to believe that the workers were starting to rise from their slumbers.

In the Neilston strike Maclean was called on to give assistance in organising and mobilising the women strikers, by local coal-miners whose daughters were involved. This was no easy task since the bulk of the women strikers were very young and inexperienced and none were in a union. For many of them the whole strike was a welcome relief from the daily round of repetitive production line work. Maclean and MacDougall were hard pressed to keep the serious nature of the dispute before the participants and to prevent the carnival atmosphere which surrounded it from taking over. But in the end the economic objectives of the strikers were largely realised and although the political gains for Maclean might have been slight, many of the women were recruited into trade unionism. At the very least, then, the Neilston strike had awakened thousands of women workers to their economic power.[11]

In the case of the Singer dispute much of the interest it generated centred on the role played by the SLP'ers who were present in the plant. As with the Neilston strike the workers most directly involved were non-union labour, women as well as men. Singer's had grown rapidly in the years preceeding 1910 until it employed some 12,000 workers at the time of the strike, of whom about a quarter were women. Virtually all the employees were unskilled and the production process was based on the very latest technology and a minute division of labour. The dispute started with a strike by some of the women against an increased work-load and soon mushroomed to the point that the whole factory was at a standstill. The small minority of ASE craftsmen continued to work until reluctantly induced to strike by a decision of their Executive Committee itself taken somewhat belatedly.

In the event the strike was defeated by a skilful and determined management who issued strikers with a 'ballot' asking them to state whether they wished to return to work or not. The implied threat to each striker was that unless they held together the management could identify all those not opting to return to work and take appropriate action against them. In effect this 'ballot' undermined the solidarity and confidence of the workers and broke the strike. In the short run the main casualties of the defeat were the SLP activists who were dismissed and dispersed around the Clydeside region. But many were to reappear as delegates to the Clyde Workers' Committee which emerged in the war.[12]

Maclean saw the Singer strike as significant for a number of reasons. The company itself was at the forefront of technological and managerial innovation. The elimination of skill through a combination of new mechanised processes and scientific division of labour was seen by Maclean as indicative of the changes which he expected to develop more generally throughout industry as a whole. Such a development required an imaginative response from trade unions used to organising on the basis of common but restricted skills. This was going to be increasingly more difficult to sustain as de-skilling became more prevalent as Maclean it was certain it would. Instead unions would have to amalgamate across craft and gender differences and begin to organise those workers they had previously ignored. This latter development Maclean saw as not only inevitable but desirable in terms of building up class solidarity and increasing political consciousness. The company tactic of using a ballot of its employees to break the dispute also led Maclean to emphasise the need for workers to make use of the secret ballot at Parliamentary elections.[13]

While the Scottish disputes attracted Maclean's interest and often his active involvement they were still localised in character. What Maclean seemed to be searching for was an issue or cause which might unite a more broadly based body of workers and raise questions of a recognisably political kind. In 1911 and 1912 the coal strikes involving tens of thousands of workers offered such a possibility. Maclean made one of his rare excursions from Scotland in the summer of 1911, travelling to the Rhondda Valley to observe at first hand the bitter struggle taking place between the South Wales Miners and the Cambrian Combine Company. This dispute, in an area where industrial militancy had grown over the previous decade, was initiated by a movement of younger rank-and-file activists influenced by syndicalist ideas. It was from this group (which included Noah Ablett and Will Mainwaring) that the influential document of the new industrial politics, 'The Miners' Next Step', was to come.[14]

Maclean stayed in the Rhondda for a week and recorded his thoughts on the dispute in *Justice*, noting with keen disappointment the failure of Scottish miners to engage in any kind of solidarity with their Welsh colleagues.[15] In one sense the Cambrian dispute was a normal kind of industrial dispute centred narrowly on the economic question of wage levels, but it involved a political dimension arising from the question of abnormal coal sources. Maclean's interest was in the search for clues as to how such disputes could be turned to engage wider political questions. Positive signs could be gleaned from the fact that it was a dispute which clearly had its origins in a rank-and-file revolt, conducted in a manner and with a vocabulary which involved the raising of revolutionary or at least quasi-revolutionary slogans and demands, and seemed to presage the possibility of a national mining dispute in the near future.

In fact such a dispute did take place in 1912, with limited success in terms of a national minimum wage, but while a national strike could be seen as an advance on a local dispute it was still limited to an occupational group and, notwithstanding its possible political undertones, was essentially sectional in character. Maclean was concerned to mobilise the widest possible action across occupational lines and was clearly already looking for issues which would involve political questions. It is in this context that an article published in *Justice* in January 1913 was written. In it Maclean wrote:

> It is now our duty to try and direct the aroused workers not only to strike for an unstable temporary advance but to concentrate at the same time on a legally fixed, definite minimum below which no adult's wage must fall. It would have to be an upwards adjustable minimum, rising with every increase in prices and increased productivity. That the state would not grant this is a foregone conclusion

... But that is all the more reason why we should fight. If we get the masses behind us, every capitalist resistance will bring us nearer the revolution.[16]

This type of attempt to construct a broad front, with its shades of a transitional programme about it, was something to which Maclean returned in the immediate post-war years.

Much of the current industrial unrest was associated with the spread of syndicalist ideas, and Maclean must have been touched by such ideas during his visit to the Rhondda, where he apparently established contact with Noah Ablett, A. J. Cook and Will Mainwaring, who were advocates of industrial unionism. Interestingly enough, William Knox asserts that Maclean's collaborator James MacDougall was profoundly influenced by syndicalist notions at this time and we know that another associate, Willie Gallacher, was likewise influenced, though probably not until he went briefly to work in Chicago.[19] But Maclean appeared to reject forcefully the syndicalist approach, talking derisively of 'anarchist unionism under the stunning title of syndicalism' and expressing relief that Scottish workers remained uncontaminated by the 'virus'.[18]

Yet on more careful examination the distance between Maclean and many advocates of Industrial Unionism, who would have described themselves as syndicalists, may not have been as wide as at first sight. Syndicalism covered a multitude of positions, from those with a very clear commitment to the syndicalist prescription of building up independent revolutionary unions, rejecting the role of politics and opposing the concept of the State to those who saw it more simply as a means of conducting a more vigorous struggle against the capitalists than the socialist parties were currently able to undertake. Maclean's position was stated most fully and clearly in April 1911, directly after the defeat of the Singer strike. Instead of castigating the SLP'ers for engaging in an absurd bout of mindless industrial anarchy he was concerned to point out that:

> All social democrats are industrial unionists. We differ from others
> in that we insist real industrial organisation must arise out of the
> fusion and federation of already existing Trade Unions ... We
> rightly insist that economic organisation is subject to political organ-
> isation ... [through] a party representative of the interests of the
> workers as a whole.[19]

Social democrats, as opposed to 'pure' syndicalists, upheld the
concept of 'the naturalness of the state and politics ... The State
is the natural outgrowth of a growing economic structure of
expanding society ... it is only consistent with impartial scientific
survey to carry forward this growth of the duties of the state
until the social revolution has been accomplished.'[20]

Such a series of propositions would have been acceptable to
many self-styled syndicalists when the practical political importance of industrial struggle was given the kind of weight in social
democratic politics which Maclean was clearly prepared to give
it. Maclean may not have been unique among social democrats
in his emphasis on the growing relevance of industrial struggle
to social transformation, but few gave as much practical support
to industrial conflicts in this whole period. And certainly few
would enter the First World War with such a flexible, positive
view as to the revolutionary possibilities offered by the emergence
of industrial uncertainty, tension and unrest.

A strike which casts some interesting light on Maclean's views
about the nature of trade unionism and syndicalism at this time
was the complex and highly unusual dispute involving the Coalburn Co-operative Society, the Lanarkshire Miners and the
National Union of Distributive and Allied Workers (NUDAW).[21]
Coalburn was a pit village in the Lanarkshire coalfield within
which the local co-operative society was dominated by miners.
It was a village with a militant image well known to both Maclean
and MacDougall who spoke there often. The initial dispute took

place when the Co-operative Directors, members of the miners' union, dismissed two employees of the co-operative for inefficiency. Members of the NUDAW, to which the two dismissed men belonged, then came out on strike, whereupon the quarterly meeting of co-operators composed almost entirely of working miners endorsed the decision of their Directors and empowered them to replace the striking employees.

At this point the NUDAW Executive called on the Lanarkshire Miners' Union to expel the Co-operative Directors for strike-breaking, a request which was accepted by the Miners' Executive. Robert Smillie, the charismatic and highly regarded leader of the Scottish miners, was despatched to Coalburn to defend the expulsions before a mass meeting of miners and was confronted by Maclean and MacDougall who came to defend the Directors. In answer to Smillie's assertion that the Directors had acted in a manner contrary to the accepted principles of trade unionism, Maclean firmly demurred. For him this was not a normal trade dispute to be judged by normal standards but a special case, where the leaders of a working-class community, with the support of the overwhelming majority of that community, had decided on a particular course of action. Maclean was not particularly concerned with the rights and wrongs of the situation but with the right of the majority to impose its will. When he was accused by ILP'ers and other defenders of trade unionism of supporting 'strike-breakers' his response was typically caustic:

As I find the average trade union as defective in outlook as any Co-operative Society, and the average trade unionist as great a mixture of virtue and vice as the average co-operator, I might respond . . . by denouncing the tuppenny-ha'penny peddling and pottering largely lauded in the name of trade unionism. If I believed the employers inside a homogeneous State or community, such as exists in Coalburn, had the supreme claim I would be an out and out Syndicalist. That, so far, I have failed to become, and so I am driven back to stand by the majority against the minority.[22]

Thus while Maclean enthusiastically adapted his social democratic practice to take on board the revolutionary possibilities offered by industrial militancy, he clearly believed this could only prove worthwhile if such militancy was informed and directed by political knowledge and understanding. This was not to be provided by a vanguard party, along Leninist lines, but by an informed working class. For Maclean, it was imperative to bring the Marxist message to a wider working class audience to ensure that industrial militancy could mature into revolutionary consciousness. As a good social democrat this meant the usual round of street-corner propaganda and the like but also, in Maclean's case, it involved a more formal commitment to the systematic development and provision of Marxist education in the fields of economics and industrial history. Maclean, assisted initially by James MacDougall and later also by Malcolm McCall and William McLaine, with special lectures by William Watson, built up a considerable reputation as a teacher of Marxist economics.[23]

The best attended classes took place in, or around Glasgow, but Maclean and MacDougall both developed classes in various towns and pit villages in the Fife and Lanarkshire coalfields. Maclean was determined to create a Scottish Labour College which would act as the educational dynamo to spark Scottish workers towards the goal of social revolution. This meant pressurising the Scottish trade unions, especially the miners, as well as the co-operatives, to support such an initiative. Much of the work in this area devolved on MacDougall who began to assume the more prominent role of the two in working within the co-operatives.

MacDougall lost no opportunity to urge upon the co-operatives the necessity of developing a Marxist-based programme of economics teaching, arguing that there was a real desire for such teaching on the part of younger-class working men. He made this point most forcefully at the Annual Co-operative Congress held in Dublin in 1914. In a discussion concerned with the issue of the co-operatives' educational programme MacDougall asserted that it was of the 'utmost importance that they should take care that the economics that were taught were from the point of view of the working classes . . . and as such must be the economics of Marx and his successors'.[24]

Such a proposition, made at a Congress presided over by a Jesuit Priest, T. Findley, and aimed at an audience still unwilling even to enter a formal relationship with the Labour Party, was unlikely to be well received. The idea that the co-operative movement as a whole would endorse a policy of supporting economics classes taught explicitly and exclusively from a Marxist point of view was clearly utopian. However, Maclean and MacDougall did mount such classes for the Greenock and Clydebank societies before the war but this was an unusual occurrence which may have owed something paradoxically to the significant role of ILP'ers in those societies.

Certainly Maclean had few illusions about the true political character of the average co-operative activist but he nonetheless continued to raise the socialist case wherever possible. His immediate preoccupation was to encourage the co-operatives to enter into formal contacts with the wider labour movement, but the high point of his relations with the co-operative movement in Scotland came in late 1911, when he read a paper to the Renfrewshire Conference at Paisley on the subject 'The Rise in the Price of Food Stuffs and Co-operation'.

This paper was published in the *Scottish Co-operator*[25] and subsequently as a pamphlet, and is particularly interesting in that it pulled together two issues which had exercised Maclean's thoughts for some time, namely the question of what caused prices to rise, and how could the co-operatives respond to the challenge of the emerging multiple retailer? Maclean began by arguing that co-operative retailers were able to flourish up to the present because they were confronted by old-style single traders who were incapable of resisting the power of the co-operative organisative. But, Maclean observed, just as modern-day industrial capital was evolving in the form of trusts and monopolies, so the private retail trade was evolving, with the small retailer being replaced by the multiple outlets who had grown to the point of posing a mortal threat to the co-operative movement.

The rise of the multiple retailer was accompanied, in time, by a fall in the price of commodities. Maclean argued, on the basis of reading official statistics and orthodox political economists, that prices had been rising steadily since 1896, reversing the previous tendency for commodity prices to fall. He asserted that by 1911 statistics indicated that commodity prices, on average, were fifteen to twenty per cent above the 1896 level and attributed this mainly to the growing output of gold. He deduced that since such prices were expressed in terms of gold, and since gold was itself falling in value relative to other articles as more gold was produced, then commodity prices would rise and indeed continue to rise in the forseeable future. At the same time wages would not increase at as fast a rate as prices, and Maclean asserted that when trade again deteriorated such wage advances as had occurred in the recent past would be reversed rapidly. This situation of rising prices and relatively lower wages played into the hands of the multiple retailers, who were able to undercut the co-operatives on the prices of many staple commodities and thereby attract away many co-operators.

Maclean pointed out that the multiples were also manufacturing their own goods and manufacturers were also moving into the retail sector to push their own products. Once the small trader had been destroyed, as seemed inevitable, the real struggle

would take place between the co-operatives and the large multiples. The fact that the co-operatives were still improving their
own position should not induce a complacent view for to 'leave
well enough alone in face of a rapidly-growing menace was
nothing short of suicide'.[26] The multiples were expanding more
rapidly than the co-operatives and in the ensuing struggle
between the multiples, the independents and the co-operatives
prices would be driven down and the surviving non-co-operative
units would combine into even larger and more powerful com-
bines. The need was for more discussion, research and experiment, for unless they evolved an appropriate strategy Maclean
saw the co-operatives facing the an unprecedented disaster. In his
view it was imperative that co-operatives began a price war
funded by increased depreciation of plant at the expense of co-
operative dividends. They should also press for the nationalisation
of transit, land and mines as an act of self-defence to prevent
capitalists from manipulating the transport system or cornering
the market in raw materials against the co-operatives. Since
capitalists fought each other by such methods in America and
Britain it was foolish to believe the co-operatives would fare any
better. Indeed they already had the example of the Glasgow meat
markets which were closed to co-operatives. To ensure an
adequate supply of commodities the co-operatives needed to
extend the production of manufactured goods and build up a
network of co-operative associations of farmers. Above all he
urged the gradual establishment of a national society which would
be better able to bring co-operative methods up to date and
provide the only means of meeting the inevitable challenge from
nationally-based multiple retailers. Maclean finally reiterated his
optimistic belief in a better future:

> The workers were going to win by means of socialism, even should
> co-operation go under. But they could not afford to let this great

movement sink before the opposition of a class that, having fulfilled its function, must inevitably yield to the workers. Just as the trade unions were performing their part, so must co-operation perform its in the great impulse towards the . . . worldwide co-operative commonwealth.[27]

At the conclusion of his talk Maclean sat down to loud appaulse before the Conference discussed the paper. Mr William Wright, the Scottish Co-operative Wholesale Society propaganda agent, felt that a proper discussion required the paper to be printed and circulated and this was approved at the end of the discussion on the recommendation of a delegate, Mr A. Holmes, from the Barrhead Society. While the paper was generally very well received it is interesting that the issue of reducing or removing the dividend excited most comment, with no speaker supporting Maclean's position on this sensitive issue. But Maclean's talk certainly impressed the Conference with its careful argument and attempt to base his analysis on empirical observation. With the exception of his final declaration of faith in a future society based on the triumph of the socialist impulse, the speech, though radical in content and aim, transcended obvious political dogma which may have helped its reception. For Maclean it was always important to connect the activities of the co-operatives to the wider socialist movement. MacDougall, drawing on Maclean's work, made this point at the Co-operative Congress in 1914 during the discussion of the report of a co-operative committee investigating the causes of the rise in commodity prices. The report 'showed the limitation of the Co-operative movement . . . to control such a vital matter . . . Co-operation was working within the limits of the competitive system; but it must march out of the competitive system into Socialism. Co-operation was only servicable in so far as it served to aid the forward movement towards that goal.'[28] However, the initial problem was how to draw the co-operatives into a closer relationship with socialist organisations or even working-class organisations like the Labour Party and the trade unions.

As we observed earlier Maclean had been present at the 1905 Co-operative Congress which had rejected a move to establish formal political contact with the Labour Party. Now in 1913 the issue was to be discussed again at the Aberdeen Congress and Maclean commented on the background and possiblities in *Justice*. His analysis is the more interesting because it expresses his general frustration with the current state of social democratic politics as well as his acknowledgement of the positive role being played within the Co-operative movement by the ILP which contrasted with the opportunities missed by social democrats. Maclean began by noting that the co-operative movement had been assisting strikes with 'fair' sums of money in recent years. He argued that the sums could have been greater had socialists and trade unionists been more aware of the possibilities offered by the co-operative movement:

> Let our men devote a tenth of the energy they have spent in modernising the trade unions and they will be surprised at the results. The I.L.P have systematically saturated all committees and associations inside the co-operative movement with the result that the leaders are invited to speak all over the country . . . and they will achieve their end sooner or later. I do admire their persistence and insistence. Had we been alert enough we might have had a resolution asking the Co-operative movement to join with the BSP. That . . .would have been a joke as the BSP, at present, hardly knows where it is, what with Militarism, Suffragettism, and Syndicalism. Until we settle affairs inside our ranks we can hardly have the face to ask such a body, as the co-operative movement to join in with us, can we really?[29]

Here we have the clearest evidence of Maclean's bitter disappointment with the current state of the BSP. It is perhaps significant that it was made in the same month, May 1913, that Maclean and MacDougall launched *The Vanguard* – the organ of the BSP Scottish branches. Through this newspaper Maclean could proclaim his political message in Scotland, and although the newspaper collapsed relatively quickly it was a technique he applied on the two subsequent occasions, when he found himself profoundly disaffected from the national leadership and policy of the party.

At one level the BSP had partially clarified its position on the controversial naval question with Hyndman's defeat in a party referendum and his subsequent resignation as Chairman. But the Party's position on the substantive naval question was equivocal in that members could exercise their individual consciences. Moreover, because of his financial control of *Justice* Hyndman was able to maintain effective control over its editorial content, though alternative opinions to his own were not excluded. However, the relationship between Party and *Justice* was becoming an issue of debate and this was the point where Maclean's voice was first raised in the BSP's national councils.

The collapse of the *Vanguard* in contrast to the growing strength of *Forward* indicated the relative strength of the BSP *vis-à-vis* the ILP in the west of Scotland.[30] We have observed that the creation of the BSP in 1911-12 fell some way short of the 'Socialist Unity' hoped for by many social democrats at the time. On Clydeside the BSP was almost entirely composed of the old SDP, with hardly any additions from the ILP despite, or perhaps because the Glasgow ILP was becoming more left-wing, even 'Marxist' in outlook. This created a curious relationship in that both parties sought to maintain separate, distinct identities although on virtually every important policy issue their views converged. In practice the lack of substantive policy differences was compensated for by the intense polemics involved on those quesions which might divide them. And it is widely assumed that Clydeside politics at this time were characterised by sectarianism. There is something in such a characterisation, but it needs to be tempered by the recollections of some participants who recall this as a period when groups could debate and argue with each other while maintaining a general atmosphere of fraternalism.

Maclean is certainly one against whom the charge of sectarianism is often levelled and yet, in practice, he was always willing to support ILP'ers who stood on socialist platforms or proclaimed the socialist case in an uncompromising way. While he was deeply critical of the ILP for its refusal to join with the BSP he did not believe they were more to be condemned than non-socialists; just the reverse. Such criticisms as he made were framed within the borders of a shared socialist identity, but provided they articulated that socialism in a straightforward manner Maclean could always be relied on to assist their efforts. One such area concerned housing policy. Any socialist on Clydeside was bound to take an interest in the housing question, which was the most important manifestation of material deprivation in the region. Maclean had long interested himself in this subject, as had ILP'ers, most notably John Wheatley, their most creative and competent political leader in Glasgow.

In October 1913 the Glasgow ILP issued a pamphlet drawn up by Wheatley which argued that the main obstacle to the construction of good housing for low rent was not the cost of land, labour or materials but the cost of capital; the interest to be repaid on the capital sum borrowed. He proposed that by using the surplus profit made by the municipal tram system, Glasgow Corporation could build homes relatively cheaply which could in turn be let at low rents. This was a general approach which Maclean had urged previously, based on the shared proposition that interest repayments constituted the 'real' cost involved, and the problem to be solved, in dealing with a programme of publicly funded house-building.

Once Wheatley's policy had been published Maclean pointed out the similarities between his own and Wheatley's approach while emphasising that they had worked on their ideas independently. He went on to urge 'our comrades' to get copies of the Wheatley pamphlet to be used in bringing the housing question to the centre of the local political stage.[31] This issue above all was one where Maclean worked closely with ILP'ers, cooperators and trade unionists on a common front and in a manner which was to climax with resounding effect during the war.

Following on from this endorsement of the Wheatley policy Maclean expressed his approval of and support for Tom Gibb, who was standing for the Labour Party at a by-election in South Lanark. Although Gibb was not a Marxist he had declared his intention in *Forward* to fight the election as an out and out socialist and it was this declaration which Maclean warmly applauded. He went on to urge BSP'ers to give as much help to Gibb's campaign as possible and pointed out that he and other BSP'ers had already worked on a joint socialist propaganda campaign in the constituency with members of the Douglas Water ILP branch, 'who are good Socialists every man of them'.[32]

For Maclean, then, the key dividing-line in politics was between socialists and non-socialists and it was the duty of socialists to support each other regardless of party. It was also their duty to criticise 'the acts of commission and omission of the Labour Party', a duty which seemed to become even more relevant to BSP'ers following their decision to seek affiliation to the Party in June 1914. Before that Maclean had attended the Easter conference of the BSP where he had joined with Peter Petroff in an attempt to impose a form of discipline on BSP candidates at elections and to wrest control of *Justice* from Hyndman. Maclean wanted *Justice* to come under the control of the BSP through a system of elected trustees and an elected editor. In such a way the newspaper would reflect more faithfully the policies of the Party rather than, as at present, the perspective of Hyndman.[33]

This issue had been raised in the past but now assumed even more importance in the light of the widening rift between Hyndman and the bulk of the BSP. In the absence of an alternative newspaper it was seen as important by Maclean to gain control of the one which was generally accepted at large as the BSP's mouthpiece. This attempt was successfully resisted by Hyndman. Maclean and Petroff also failed in their attempt to ensure that all BSP candidates standing for election to public bodies should stand on a common programme laid down by the Party. Additional information designed to meet particular local circumstances would be permitted but only when it was circulated as a distinct leaflet or document. It could not be included as part of the Party programme. That such a resolution could not pass through the BSP Conference in 1914 suggests how far it was from any concepion of a vanguard or tightly disciplined organisation. Yet many of the same delegates would welcome the Bolshevik Revolution and apparently embrace wholeheartedly a conception of the revolutionary party which they could scarcely, indeed in most cases could not comprehend. But before then social democracy was to meet its nemesis in the form of the war.

4 War hero

When war broke out in August 1914 John Maclean had already spent more than ten years in the service of the social democratic cause. In that time he had addressed hundreds of meetings throughout Scotland, actively participated in the co-operative movement and had developed an expanding programme of more formally based Marxist education classes. Neither his work as a school teacher nor marriage and children deflected him from his political commitments which he pursued with energy and ability. Maclean's dedicated role in the public dissemination of the social democratic analysis of and prescriptions for British society was not without its rewards.

By 1914 his education classes based on Marxism were starting to attract comparatively large audiences of workers and he had established something of a reputation as a Marxist propagandist. But it was a modest reputation in the sense that he remained largely unkown to the mass of Scottish workers outside the small group of socialist and trade union activists attracted by his classes. Beyond Scotland Maclean was largely unknown even to many involved in socialist politics and the wider Labour Movement. Social democrats might know him as the author of Scottish Notes in *Justice* and be aware of his other contributions to that newspaper but on the whole he was not an individual with whom most would be familiar. Maclean held no official position in the SDP and had never been a member of its Executive. Indeed he rarely attended the annual party conferences and had only latterly participated in debates at the national level. He was, in short, a relatively unknown socialist operating within a party which enjoyed little popular support in Britain and even less in Scotland.

Ten years of sustained and enthusiastic agitation by Maclean and other socialists, both social democrats and ILP'ers, had scarcely dented, let alone breached the traditionally strong wall of radical, working-class liberalism which characterised Clydeside and Scottish politics. Certainly there were few indications before 1914 that Clydeside would become synonymous in the public mind with socialist politics. But the war was to produce this transformation and much more besides.

In Maclean's case the war was to effect a dramatic alteration in his political status. From a position of relative political obscurity Maclean was to become an object of discussion at Cabinet level and a constant source of concern for the Scottish office. If we exclude Sinn Feiners he became Britain's most important political prisoner of the war and as such assumed the role of socialist hero-martyr or 'folk-devil' depending on the point of view. After the Bolshevik Revolution Maclean's appointment as Soviet Consul in Glasgow caused consternation in the Foreign Office and underlined the regard with which he was held by the Bolsheviks.[1] Indeed Lenin had commented on Maclean's dedication to the Internationalist cause on a number of occasions and clearly saw him as the man around whom a new revolutionary party could be built in Britain.

This transformation in status was accomplished through Maclean's opposition to the war and espousal of an Internationalist revolutionary socialist politics. It involved three periods of imprisonment during the war which have led to a controversy about Maclean's treatment by the authorities and to questions about his subsequent mental state. Clearly for Maclean, as for many others, the war was both a trial and a watershed in his personal and political development.

Although the prospect of a war involving the European Powers had been widely predicted and anticipated before 1914 the actual outbreak of hostilities in that summer came as a shock. More profoundly shocking for socialists was the sight of socialist parties in the belligerent countries committing themselves to the various 'national' causes after the briefest of hesitations. The socialist belief in international working-class brotherhood, enshrined in the anti-war resulutions solemnly proclaimed by The International, was exposed as illusory and the gap between socialist theory and practice, on this most profound of all issues, turned out to be an unbridgeable gulf.

In Britain all socialist and working-class organisations were divided, with the ILP best able to adopt an anti-war posture based on a principled pacifism, shared with some Liberal political figures and derived from a similar pool of radicalism. For social democrats such a pacifist attitude was less readily available. The faction of the BSP led by Hyndman, and including most of the veteran party figures and key office-holders, argued that the British war effort should be supported. They cited Marx and Engels as endorsing the view that war could be justified in certain circumstances and declared that German aggression against Belgium demonstrated the bestial and reactionary character of the 'Junker State' which had to be resisted. The only way of combating such autocratic, politically regressive and militaristic conduct was war.[2] Thus the BSP Executive urged its members to give active support to the war effort, including the participation of Party spokesman on recruitment platforms, providing that they were free at the same time, to put forward the BSP's general political programme.[3] This Executive instruction led to considerable controversy within the Party and a meeting of the London branches repudiated it by an overwhelming margin.[4] It would be wrong to think that the struggle within the BSP was divided neatly between pro and anti-war factions. In fact there were a series of positions available to social democrats between these two extreme poles and it is likely that most social democrats were to be found in this 'in-between' area. In so far as any meaningful description can be given to the general position occupied by most social democrats it would be 'defencist'. 'Defencism' allowed social democrats to support the war as an act of self-defence against German aggression while opposing the idea that territory or other advantages should accrue from the war. Thus 'defencists' could support the war without engaging in the kind of jingoistic excess associated with the Hyndmanites. This approach, typical of the general perspective of social democrats throughout the belligerent powers was flexible and elastic enough to be stretched in various directions to cover most eventualities. It also allowed its adherents to maintain the view that their actions were still consistent with a Marxist approach. This was not a position which Maclean entertained.

Maclean was on a family holiday in Tarbert in the Scottish Highlands when war was declared. His immediate response was to engage in a bout of anti-war graffiti in Tarbert.[5] A more careful exposition of his views was provided in *Justice* in September 1914 where he argued that the war could not be supported on any terms. He rejected the idea that British entry into the war had much to do with the German violation of Belgian neutrality. Maclean saw this as a pretext and asserted that the war was actually a part of the struggle for territorial gain and markets by the great powers. It was a struggle 'on a capitalist national scale' which could not provide a justification for workers enlisting in the armies of national capitalism, still less for socialists to support such enlistment. If Germany was engaged in an expansionist and aggressive policy Maclean saw the German socialist and working-class movement as the appropriate antidote. Moreover he went on to predict that the war would not produce a settlement of the differences between the capitalist states at its conclusion. Rather it would fuel a further burst of rivalries and annexations between the capitalist powers including Russia, Japan, America and even China unless social revolution broke out in Europe.[6]

This was an interesting analysis both as a statement framed in the tenets of what had been social democratic orthodoxy and as an indication of Maclean's tendency to view events in international categories. In these opening moments in a war primarily involving European powers, Maclean saw its possible impact on the future development of world capitalism, and argued the mechanism for preventing this outcome in terms of a European as opposed to a British or German revolution. But Maclean's position on the war began to develop in more radical ways as it progressed.

In effect Maclean started from an anti-war position which involved the public articulation of its causes and meaning and a call for a negotiated peace. All this took place within the accepted parameters of the established liberal freedoms, notably freedom of speech. Maclean was consciously concerned to operate within the law and when urging pressure on the government did so in a constitutional manner. He defended himself in such terms during his first two appearances before the courts, denying both the substance and evidence in charges which effectively accused him of hampering the war effort. However, Maclean ended the war having embraced the idea that all measures of political and industrial action should be taken to stop the war, even those of an illegal nature. Indeed he publicly urged British workers to emulate the example of the Bolsheviks in making a revolution. If Maclean entered the war as a social democrat he left it with a fundamentally different set of attitudes to the problem of social transformation. If not a self-conscious Leninist he certainly exhibited forms of thinking and practice reminiscent of Leninism, although it is probably more accurate to see Maclean's political trajectory as lying closer to Liebknecht and Luxemburg than Lenin.

After the start of the war Maclean seems to have continued much as before. He addressed public meetings, developed his classes in Marxist economics and industrial history and participated in the Co-operative Movement.[7] He remained especially involved in the project to create a Scottish Labour College which seemed to be moving towards realisation. Much of Maclean's practical political work in late 1914 and early 1915 was focused on the immediate social and economic consequences of the war as they impacted on the Clydeside working class. In particular he was concerned in agitations surrounding rising food prices and the problems of housing shortages as labour was sucked into the region's engineering industries.[8] In effect Maclean's earliest propaganda was a mixture of principled objection to the war as a capitalist conspiracy and practical concern with the war's effects on working-class living standards. Thus the Pollokshaws' Branch of the BSP demanded at a well attended meeting in August that the Eastwood School Board should feed the poor children in its care, and Maclean congratulated the United Co-operative Society in October for keeping down the price of bread.[9] Issues like this were popular enough but Maclean did not avoid the more difficult question of the war itself.

He was initially enouraged in his propaganda by what he saw as popular indifference in Glasgow to the war. In the previous year he had detected a growing receptivity amongst the local working class to jingo agitation but now he argued that jingo enthusiasm only existed in the popular press. This observation was also shared by the ILP newspaper *Labour Leader* which commented on the lack of any pro-war feeling amongst Glasgow workers. Certainly Maclean was able to hold regular street-corner meetings where he expounded his views on the nature and causes of the war as well as raising the regular issues of class politics. Indeed Maclean held one of the earliest anti-war meetings in Glasgow in August 1914, where he called for an immediate armistice and demanded that government control food prices and distribute food to the poor.[10]

This set the tone for Maclean's early meetings at which he emphasised that German and British workers were not enemies and that Germany alone was not responsible for the war. His most important regular meeting was held on Sunday evenings in Bath Street, close to the headquarters of the Glasgow Tramway, which was the site of Glasgow's main army recruitment office.[11] Despite the sensitive location and the nature of his message Maclean seems to have conducted his meetings in a generally orderly atmosphere. Minor disturbances occurred from time to time but the monthly meetings continued uninterrupted up to September 1915 when Maclean was first arrested.

He was also able to address a meeting of the Renfrewshire Co-operative Association in November 1914 on the subject 'The War, Its Causes and Cure'.[12] Here he outlined his thoughts on the issue before an audience of more than a hundred co-operative delegates, urging them to join with those opposed to the war in applying peaceful pressure on government to accept an armistice and sign a peace. The reception which this anti-war discourse received was cordial enough and the Association passed a vote of thanks to Maclean for his talk.

But as the war dragged on into 1915 and losses at the front began to mount the activities of anti-war agitators like Maclean assumed a more dangerous quality in the eyes of the authorities. What might be accepted as mere eccentricity and the exercise of a traditional right of free speech in 1914 was now seen as subversion. The introduction of the Defence of the Realm Act provided government with a range of measures to curtail or contain dissent and these could be amended to take account of other problems which might emerge.[13] Thus Maclean's public meetings were subject to increased and fairly overt official surveillance, with his utterances on the war noted by police officers.

Such surveillance was stepped up during 1915 when Clydeside began to exhibit the first real signs that it was becoming politically sensitive and volatile.

The source of this political volatility was not so much the war itself but the social and industrial problems which it brought in its train. In the case of Clydeside the most acute problems related to the dire shortage of adequate housing and the attempt to introduce new technology and methods into the region's engineering industry, especially those in the munitions sector. As attempts were made to increase war production so more and more labour was attracted to Clydeside with consequential effects on housing rents.[14]

The housing stock had always been inadequate and insufficient, providing socialist agitators with a consistently powerful and emotive local issue which they could exploit in certain circumstances. By the spring of 1915 the question of housing and rents had become potentially explosive as private landlords began to raise their rents in response to increased demand. Although most landlords exempted the families of combatants from the increases some did not, and this gave a particular twist to the rent campaign which developed throughout 1915.

Resistance to the rent increases began more or less spontaneously in the Govan district in May 1915 before spreading more widely. It was organised by an ILP'er, Andrew McBride, who had encouraged the formation of a Women's Housing Association in which Helen Crawfurd and Mrs Barbour played leading roles.[15] This organisation, inaugurated in the autumn of 1914 with about fifty members, had more than 3,000 members at its height and came to direct an agitation which involved some 40,000 householders.[16] Maclean and MacDougall were actively engaged in the rent agitation from its earliest days, having long concerned themselves with the housing problems of Clydeside. Indeed we have noted that before the war Maclean had urged BSP'ers to give energetic support to Wheatley's housing policy, which was in general accord with his own. Maclean continued to argue that the only way a major programme of publicly funded house building for low rent could be sustained was by removing the interest charge from the capital used. It was not the cost of land or materials which prevented such a programme but the high interest charged on loans.

But, in the present circumstances, Maclean supported the policy of withholding that portion of the rent which consisted of increases imposed since the outbreak of war. His distinctive contribution to the rent agitation was to try and secure industrial support by addressing factory gate and dockyard meetings. The agitation reached its climax in November 1915 when eighteen tenants were summoned before the Glasgow Small Debt Court for default on rent. The occasion, described as probably the greatest event in the history of the Clyde workers by Patrick Dollan, the ILP chronicler of the agitation, involved several thousand demonstrators, including striking munitions workers mostly from the Govan shipyards who downed tools and attended in support of the defaulters.[17] Maclean was present, having absented himself from his classroom in response to appeals from the demonstrators. What might have produced a disturbance was avoided by Sheriff Lee who, having consulted the Ministry of Munitions, induced the landlord to withdraw the charges against the defaulters.[18] At an impromtu meeting which followed outside the court, Maclean was asked to transmit a resolution to the Prime Minister, Herbert Asquith, on behalf of the demonstrators, requesting 'the Government to definitely state, not later than Saturday first, that it forbids any increase in rent during the period of the war, and that this failing, a general strike will be declared on Monday 22 November'.[19]

There is no record that this resolution had any effect and certainly it evoked no direct response. However, the government quickly placed a Rent Restrictions Act on the Statute Book which held rent and mortgage repayments to the level obtaining on 4 August 1914, for the duration of the war. This was seen by many as a concession wrung from a reluctant government by popular agitation. In fact it is evident that such a measure was already under active consideration by government, although the timing and speed of its implementation must have owed something to public dissatisfaction on Clydeside and throughout much of industrial Britain. Certainly Lloyd George and his ministers and officials in the recently created Ministry of Munitions were concerned to prevent problems emerging which might have an adverse effect on industrial production. Clydeside had already been subject to important industrial dislocation and unrest in the first half of 1915 and as the Ministry of Munitions prepared to speed up the introduction of unskilled labour and tighter industrial discipline in the arms production sector Lloyd George threw his considerable political weight behind the rent reform.

Maclean had seen the rent strike as evidence that the previously 'backward' Glasgow working class was becoming radicalised. He argued that the strike was the first stage in the development of the political strike which would force an end to the war.[20] It is conceivable that a conjunction between popular hostility to rent increases, growing industrial tension on Clydeside and widespread concern over the propect of conscription into the armed forces might have produced an explosive political mixture such as Maclean was seeking to promote. In the circumstances the removal of the rent issue from the political agenda eliminated a potentially dangerous source of popular disaffection. But the industrial scene still remained problematical both for the authorities and for socialist and industrial militants, watching it closely to discern the mood of the workers involved.

Industrial unrest on Clydeside was focused on the strategically important munitions sector of the engineering industry. It accounted for about a fifth of all Clydeside engineering, although much of that fifth was composed of shipbuilding. The development of the Shop Stewards Movement and the significance to be attached to it has been discussed in considerable detail in the memoirs of participants and in the various academic interpretations and disputations which exist.[21] However, it is necessary to say something about the unrest here since so much of Maclean's activity as a revolutionary was concentrated on the attempt to give industrial disputes a definite political character and revolutionary objective.

Various unions of skilled workers existed in the Clydeside engineering plants. Most were relatively small and the dominating trade union presence was supplied by the Amalgamated Society of Engineers (ASE). The ASE had been the classic example of the craft union of the mid-Victorian period; *the* new model union. It had been composed traditionally of highly skilled workers who entered the trade union through a tightly controlled system of apprenticeship. In 1897 the national position of the ASE had been undermined in a momentous industrial dispute which had practically bankrupted the union and resulted in a historic defeat. This defeat allowed employers to introduce new technology and labour methods to processes which had previously been the preserve of skilled engineers. In effect the powerful control over the production process exercised by members of the ASE was broken and technology replaced obsolete skills.

The significance of the 1897 defeat had been felt in the London and Birmingham based engineering industries but Clydeside remained almost completely untouched before the war. On Clydeside, engineers continued to enjoy the privileges of craft exclusiveness in terms of pay and conditions as well as social status. They remained an aristocracy of labour bound together by shared skills, privileges and outlook which they sought to preserve by periodic displays of ferocious militancy in defence of their sectional interests. In short they possessed a curious mixture of industrial militancy and conservatism which made them difficult to handle as both employers and their own full-time officials often found out. This defensive militancy appears to have inhibited most local employers from confronting their workforce with new methods even after the outbreak of war. This lack of innovation on the part of employers caused considerable disquiet among leading officials in the soon to be formed Ministry of Munitions.[22] However, as we shall see, not all Clydeside employers were inhibited; some saw the war as presenting an opportunity to fundamentally transform their productive methods and work practices.

The first evidence of industrial unrest began in February 1915 and concerned negotiations over district time rates of pay which had been ongoing since before the outbreak of war. An estimated 10,000 engineers struck in protest against the pay agreement concluded between the employers and the ASE leadership which fell some way short of the Unions's initial demand. This unofficial strike was condemned by the local officials of the ASE as well as the national leadership and was illegal under the terms of the DORA. The strike was led by an unofficial body of shop stewards drawn from the ASE and various other small craft unions. This body, the Clyde Labour Withholding Committee was careful to emphasise the normal industrial character of the dispute and prudently avoided the use of the word 'strike' in the Committee's title. The dispute was finally settled in March following the appointment of an agreed arbitrator, Sir George Askwith, who increased the original offer without granting the initial union demand.[23]

Although this dispute was ostensibly concerned with the normal issue of rates of pay there was evidence that it contained the seeds of more serious problems to come. William Weir, the most aggressive of the Clydeside employers, had already begun to embark on the introduction of new 'American' style methods. His most radical challenge to the ASE was the introduction of a group of American engineers, employed on a lavish bonus scheme, designed to undermine the industrial grip on production practices exercised by the union. It was a protest strike by 2,000 of Weir's employees at his Cathcart factory against this private attempt at dilution of labour which actually acted as the catalyst in bringing out the other engineers over pay in the same month, February 1915.

The Cathcart issue, although submerged in the wider pay question, gave a clear enough indication of the likely response of engineers to measures which might undermine their general industrial position. But the requirements of the war effort were imposing their own pressures and they ran counter to the sectional interests of Clydeside engineers. The prospect of an attack on the existing methods of work in this engineering processes essential to the war effort seemed inevitable and the setting up of a Ministry of Munitions in June 1915 emphasised this inevitability.[24]

By the spring of 1915 government became clear that the successful prosecution of the war required the active co-operation of organised labour. In the main trade unions had pledged their support for the war and this had been formalised in the Treasury Agreements concluded in May 1915. The effect of these Agreements was that trade unions agreed to suspend various restrictive practices and other constraints on production for the duration of the war. They also agreed to refrain from any strike action. Government undertook to ensure that wartime profiteering would be stamped out and pledged that trade unions could return to their normal work practices once the war ended. Clearly engineering was an area where co-operation was most eagerly sought and although the ASE formally accepted the Treasury Agreement there was considerable official scepticism about how enthusiastic that support was. In particular the condemnation by the ASE leadership of unofficial shop floor organisation, like the Clyde Labour Withholding Committee and later the Clyde Workers' Committee, was seen by Lloyd George's deputy, Christopher Addison, as a form of ritual hypocrisy.[25]

It is against this background that the role of the Ministry of Munitions needs to be viewed. The primary objective of the Lloyd George-led Ministry was straightforward enough, to increase the supply of vital war material to the front. The method to achieve this was the categorisation of certain factories and industrial plants as 'controlled establishments'. These establishments would be subject to ultimate direction by the Ministry and here dilution of labour would be introduced along with more rigorous industrial discipline. Workers in controlled establishments were subject to the use of leaving certificates whereby any employee leaving his work could not be re-employed elsewhere for six weeks unless they were in receipt of a leaving certificate.

This regulation was to become a particular source of friction in the months ahead. Indeed the first real problem for the Ministry concerned the use of such certificates by the Fairfield Shipyard in the case of two employees who were dismissed and refused certificates. This action produced an illegal, unofficial strike by other employees at the Fairfield Yard at what they saw as an attempt by the employer to use the leaving certificate as a disciplinary measure against awkward employees. Seventeen strikers were summoned before a Munitions Tribunal, set up under the Munitions Act, and fined. However, three were jailed after they refused to pay their fines, provoking a general storm of protest with threats of further illegal sympathetic strikes.[26]

In the summer many of those who had participated in the earlier Clyde Labour Withholding Committee had come together to create the Clyde Workers Committee (CWC) to combat the perceived threat posed by the passage of the Munitions Act with its creation of the Ministry of Munitions. The CWC rapidly assumed a key role as the voice of rank-and-file engineers in the munitions sector and although adopting a cautious attitude to the Fairfields case it nonetheless presented a potential threat which the authorities could not discount. Lloyd George responded to this awkward situation by appointing a committee of two, Lord Balfour and Lynden Macassey, to enquire into the general grievances of munitions workers and by inducing the payment of the fines on the three imprisoned defaulters by the unions concerned. With the imprisoned fine defaulters released and a special commission in place Lloyd George ensured that the CWC would not be tempted to initiate industrial action.

The Balfour–Macassey Report recommended that the Ministry should appoint Dilution Commissioners who would oversee the implementation of the dilution policy and smooth out any difficulties which might emerge.[27] But even the adoption of this recommendation did little to help the process of dilution and the evidence is clear that little progress was achieved during 1915. However official pressure was maintained on the ASE Executive to endorse the dilution policy and the Ministry armed itself with more effective legal powers to curtail the activities of industrial and political agitators.

An amendment to Regulation 42 of DORA, which concerned the offence of incitement to cause mutiny, sedition or disaffection among the forces or civilian populations, was widened to include acts designed 'to impede, delay or restrict the production, repair or transport of war material or any other work necessary for the successful prosecution of the war'.[28] This amendment was something of a 'catch all' particularly designed to catch agitators like Maclean rather than munitions workers. Despite the obstacles and likely conflicts in prospect Lloyd George determined to advance the dilution issue on Clydeside and elsewhere.

For Maclean the events of 1915, notably the industrial strikes at its start, the militant reaction to the Munitions Act and the wide-scale agitation against rent increases, seemed to represent a major advance in working-class consciousness. We have seen that he was intimately involved in the rent agitation but he also had close contact with the CWC, which spearheaded resistance to the encroachments of the Ministry of Munitions. Willie Gallacher, chairman of the CWC was a particularly close associate of Maclean and a member of the anti-war section of the BSP. Others had attended Maclean's economic classes.

But it is important not to overstate his influence upon the CWC.[29] Maclean was permitted to attend its meetings and to contribute to the debates. However, there is nothing to suggest that he influenced any important decision which the Committee arrived at. The role he played was that of a left opposition trying to encourage the CWC to adopt a more overtly political approach in its interpretation of industrial questions and specifically to oppose the war. In this he failed. The CWC never really developed beyond its original role as a defensive industrial organisation eschewing any idea that it was seeking to exercise political power or offer a criticism of the legitimacy of the war. Its failure to adopt the course prescribed for it by Maclean was not simply the result of the leadership's fear that they could not carry the rank and file down such a road. It reflected the divisions within the CWC where it is doubtful that a majority shared Maclean's opposition to the war at this stage.

Maclean had maintained his normal punishing schedule of street-corner and factory gate meetings. Together with MacDougall he had continued to develop his classes in economics and industrial history. The expansion in the number of workers attending these classes was additional encouragement to Maclean, as was the fact that his anti-war line had been carried by the Glasgow BSP if not the wider Scottish and British parties.[30] The rising level of consciousness as evidenced in the rent agitation and industrial disputes seems to have added an edge to Maclean's rhetoric. In September 1915 he was briefly arrested for making statements likely to lead to a breach of the peace and in the same month he initiated the re-launch of *The Vanguard* as the mouthpiece of the Glasgow BSP.

The Vanguard made its views on the war clear and emphasised the powerful position which workers now held and could exploit. The columns of *The Vanguard* in late 1915 and early 1916 show how far Maclean had travelled from orthodox social democracy. He was now preaching the use of the political strike to end the war and using a conception of social revolution which was closer to Lenin than Kautsky. If Sylvia Pankhurst is to be believed Maclean's public statements at this time were plainly seditious, a view which the authorities clearly shared. Although Maclean had been briefly detained by the police in September he was subsequently charged with making statements with the object of obstructing recruitment at the end of October and remanded on bail to appear before the Sheriff's Court on 10 November. Fearing a prison sentence, Maclean invited Peter Petroff to move to Glasgow to assume some of the teaching and propaganda functions which Maclean and MacDougall shared.[31]

This invitation was also motivated by concern to offer Petroff and his German wife Irma greater protection against official harassment as aliens. This was to prove a forlorn hope as both Petroffs were interned under section 14(b) of DORA in December.[32] But before this Petroff provided *The Vanguard* and Maclean with more accurate information about developments within the London based BSP Executive and the wider socialist movement on the continent. In successive issues Petroff concentrated on the Zimmerwald Conference of socialists opposed to the war which was largely ignored by the socialist press in Britain. He pointed to the Zimmerwald Manifesto as signifying a step in the right direction of constructing a new Socialist International and castigated the attempts made by the Belgian socialist Emile Vandervelde to raise money for the restoration of an 'Allied' Second International. In his final contribution before his arrest, Petroff denounced Vandervelde and the BSP Executive as deserters of the socialist cause on the outbreak of war. He specifically urged those Executive members, like E. C. Fairchild and H. W. Alexander, who opposed the Hyndmanite faction in theory, to do so in practice, and decisively:

> It is clearly impossible to support the manifesto of the Zimmerwald Conference and at the same time Vandervelde, Hyndman and company. We would suggest to those members of the Executive Committee who pose as the opposition in the BSP to sit down fast on one of the two stools between which they are wavering.[33]

Although Maclean's active partnership with Petroff lasted less than three months it was significant in a number of ways. It brought Maclean into a fuller realisation that his developing opposition to the war and approach to the idea of social revolution was shared by other European socialists. It thus reaffirmed his belief in, and commitment to Internationalism. The connection with Petroff also saw *The Vanguard* adopting a more assertive and forthright critique of the BSP Executive than before. Maclean had made no secret of his differences with the Executive but now those differences were confronted head on.

Certainly the general tone of Maclean's political propaganda was sharpened and reinforced by his discussions with Petroff, and this was reflected in their challenge to the CWC to adopt a definite anti-war stand and to channel industrial discontent in that political direction. Indeed Petroff put the point at a meeting of the Committee following the report of its secretary John Muir on the measures being taken to meet the government's attempts to impose dilution of labour. Petroff objected that Muir talked only on industrial questions and had neglected the most important issue, that of the war itself. He voiced these criticisms with such emotional fervour that Gallacher expelled him from the meeting and when MacDougall attempted to intervene in support of Petroff he too was expelled. Maclean happened to arrive at the meeting some time later to find his associates excluded from the Committee's business on the direction of Gallacher, another political ally. A sharp exchange took place between the two and relations were temporarily breached, an occurence which was to happen again with more finality.[34]

Events were now moving rapidly on a number of fronts. Maclean had appeared before Sheriff Lee on 10 November charged with making speeches designed to undermine recruitment. In answer to a heckler's call that he should enlist, Maclean had responded by announcing that he had enlisted in the socialist army and 'God damn the other army'. Maclean argued that he had in fact said 'God damn all other armies' to express his opposition to the present military system as a means of settling national disputes. He also denied saying that soldiers who killed German soldiers were murderers, pointing out that some of his dearest friends had enlisted in the British Army and were at the front. However, he did not deny allegations that he described the war as 'this murder business'.[35]

Reactions to Maclean's court appearance and conviction were interesting and varied. Sylvia Pankhurst was surprised at what she took to be the defensive, even plaintive quality of his explanation.[36] Certainly the core of Maclean's defence was couched in terms of the liberal conception of free speech and his defence was organised by a Free Speech Committee, formed after his arrest. Perhaps the strength of Liberal ideas at all levels in Scottish society accounts for the surprisingly slight sentence imposed by Sheriff Lee. Lee initially levied a fine of £5 and, when Maclean indicated that he would refuse to pay, substituted five days' imprisonment. But even then Lee allowed Maclean seven days in which to reconsider his action.[37] At almost the same time an ILP'er, James Houston, a schoolteacher, was fined £10 in Ayr for a similar offence. While Houston paid the fine, Maclean chose to serve the five days.[38]

While Sylvia Pankhurst thought Maclean's defence tame, some of the veteran social democrats associated with Hyndman were appalled. Dan Irving, one of the best known BSP'ers, wrote to the *Manchester Guardian*: 'I view Maclean's statement and the evidence given on his behalf as a libel on the BSP . . . and . . . desire publicly to disassociate the Party and certainly myself from such a scandalous imputation'.[39] This drew a response from Malcolm MacColl, who worked as part of Maclean's economics and industrial teaching team in Glasgow. MacColl protested to *Justice*: 'If Dan Irving does not make amends for his uncharitable condemnation some of us must regard him as a deserter from International Social Democracy.'[40] But this cut little ice with the Hyndmanites and H. J. Kebbell, an active social democrat for twenty years, replied to MacColl in sharp terms. He supported strongly Irving's view and asked 'whether the times are not very much too serious for us any longer to defend members who mistake licence for liberty'.[41]

Closer to home Maclean also saw his defence provoke criticism. 'A Soldier's Wife' writing in *The Scottish Co-operator* objected to his inclusion on the panel of those teaching public speaking. It was, she wrote 'an insult to those who have given their nearest and dearest'.[42] Maclean had still been active in co-operative circles up to September 1915 but after his November imprisonment his active association with that movement began to weaken. At about this time his career as a schoolteacher came to an end in confusing and controversial circumstances which reveal something about Maclean's personality.

Maclean was a well regarded schoolteacher who took his duties seriously. However, he had a history of disputes with the educational authorities and had already moved schools on a number of occasions. Throughout much of 1915 he had been involved in a running battle with his headmaster at Lambhill Street School, Mr Hugh Fulton. A number of allegations were made against Fulton but at the core was an assertion that he was involved in a relationship with a young infant schoolmistress who was effectively carrying out some of his official functions and responsibilities. When the Board investigated the various allegations made by Maclean they found no basis for them and decided to transfer him to yet another school. There matters might have ended, except that Maclean wrote a typically pugnacious letter to the Board protesting against their decision and reiterating the original allegations against Fulton. It was his refusal to withdraw these allegations unreservedly and not his political views which the Board gave in defence of their action to dismiss him.[43] It is doubtful that this was the whole truth given the experience of other schoolteachers who expressed opposition to the war and were dismissed. James Maxton and James Houston are two such, and Maclean seems a third. Certainly Maclean's behaviour in the circumstances seems reckless in the extreme, reflecting his awkwardness and rather old-fashioned sense of honour which produced an unbending determination to pursue what he believed to be right, regardless of the personal consequences which might follow. In this case Maclean lost his career and never worked as a schoolteacher again. He was more fully than ever what he had really been all his adult life – a professional revolutionary.

When Maclean emerged from his five-day imprisonment at the end of November 1915 the rent strike had begun to damp down in the face of the government's imposition of rent control. The creation of a Scottish National Housing Association at the start of 1916 was its immediate political legacy, designed to continue the longer-term campaign for a massive programme of publicly owned rented accommodation based on the Wheatley scheme. Maclean was elected as the Association's secretary but events on the industrial front, particularly the government's determination to achieve a rapid expansion in arms production through a dilution of labour scheme, overshadowed all else except the proposals to introduce conscription.

The prospect of conscription was bound to be viewed critically in a Liberal city like Glasgow where the values of liberal–radicalism were deeply ingrained. This issue more than any other tipped the balance in the BSP against the war and produced a movement towards determined opposition amongst socialists, in all groups, who had wavered on the issue. For munitions workers on Clydeside the conjunction of the dilution and conscription issues was seen as posing a direct threat to trade union orgnisation. Events were moving quickly as the government attempted to prepare the ground for its dilution proposals. Evidence of the importance which was attached to smooth implementation was the decision of Lloyd George to visit Clydeside in December and to meet the shop stewards and the rank and file. The clear assumption was that he could effect the breakthrough by force of personality and acute political skill.[44]

The Ministry of Munitions had been collating information from various sources on the state of feeling on Clydeside for some time in order to balance the appropriate mix of concessions and coercion necessary to get dilution through. One piece of advice from its principal industrial adviser warned that any precipitate action against members of the CWC might set off a concerted strike. However, action against Petroff and Maclean was recommended as the obvious first move to test the water and undermine the militants. It was doubted that the arrest of the likes of Petroff or Maclean would produce any serious reaction from the rank-and-file engineers.[45] Petroff was, in fact, detained in December 1915 and formally interned under DORA from 3

January 1916.[46]

His detention coincided with a brief insertion in *Justice* entitled 'Who and What Is Peter Petroff?' which advised workers on Clydeside to question the motives behind Petroff's presence in the area.[47] This drew a denunciation from George Chicherin on behalf of the RSDLP who pointed out that such an accusation placed Petroff in the most serious danger.[48] Maclean responded even more fiercely in a letter to *Justice* on 30 December. In what turned out to be his final contact with that newspaper he pointed out that neither he nor his associates were dictated to by Petroff, but that Petroff was working under their direction. They also shared the view that Vandervelde was a traitor to socialism and that he was partly responsible for the breakdown of the International. As if to signal the final breach with the Hyndmanites and in an echo of the accusation against Petroff Maclean wrote, 'Some of us in Glasgow have been asking, who and what are Messrs Hyndman, Bax, Fisher, Hunter, Watts, etc?'[49] Maclean was to maintain a concerted campaign against the internments of both Peter and Irma Petroff and later against that of Chicherin. Notes of protest from various Scottish-based trade unions, which were received by the Home Office, were 'all traceable to John Maclean'.[50] Maclean was prohibited from communicating with Chicherin and the Petroffs and his letters were intercepted. He never met Petroff after the latter's internment and had little direct contact with him thereafter.

While Maclean was obviously concerned about the detention of the Petroffs the major political event on Clydeside at this time was the visit of Lloyd George, designed to pacify the engineers. He toured some of the key munitions factories prior to a large-scale meeting with shop stewards at the St Andrew's Hall on Christmas Day. In fact reaction to the policy of dilution was more complex than might have seemed the case at first sight. It is probable that most rank and file supporters of the CWC were instinctively opposed to dilution. However, the syndicalist leadership were not opposed to the principle and indeed favoured it as a way of breaking down the sectional barriers which divided workers. In practice they demanded some measure of control over the implementation of dilution and stricter controls over the role of private enterprise. They were moving towards a policy of workers' control to replace the older concept of individual craft control which was the central instinct of Clydeside engineers.

Maclean had long favoured a policy of dilution, believing that the ASE needed to expand its membership to include the unskilled and semi-skilled workers who were a growing phenomenon in the engineering trade as new technology inevitably gained ground. But in the present situation he opposed dilution precisely because it would improve arms production and hence the war effort. He pointed out to Gallacher that it was a contradiction to oppose the war while effectively negotiating with the authorities to increase the amount of munitions to be deployed at the front.

Lloyd George's visit to Clydeside turned out to be unsuccessful. His meeting in the St Andrew's Hall at which he was accompanied by the Labour leader, Arthur Henderson, provoked a noisy response from his audience, with Maclean's supporters well to the fore. Indeed the mission to pacify Clydeside was such a disaster that press reports of the St Andrew's Hall meeting were officially censored. But a full account of the proceedings was carried in the New Year's Day edition of *Forward* which had not been notified of the censorship decision. As a result the police raided the offices of *Forward* and its printing presses, confiscating copies of the offending edition as well as proofs of Maclean's *Vanguard* which were being prepared for publication.[51] *Forward* was briefly subject to a ban on publication but *Vanguard* did not appear again for the duration of the war. The incidental seizure of the more seditious *Vanguard* alerted the authorities to the full extent and range of oppositional arguments circulating within the militant movement and beyond to the wider working class on Clydeside. It served to raise Maclean's political profile as one of the most dangerous and seditious agitators at large.

The failure of Lloyd George's mission saw the authorities embark on a more determined assault on the militants and revolutionary socialists. Maclean was arrested in early February 1916 and held for a week in Edinburgh Castle before being charged to appear before the High Court. The charge related to public utterances made to munitions workers which fell within the amended regulation of DORA dealing with the offence of inducing others to obstruct the war effort. Although Maclean was released on bail pending his trial, the initial incarceration in Edinburgh meant that he missed the foundation conference of the Scottish Labour College. James MacDougall read out the statement which Maclean had intended to deliver, with its emphasis on the need for workers to develop their own specialised system of education to reflect their class interests.[52] While Maclean urged that Marxist economics should be the cornerstone of the curriculum he observed that skills in writing, basic mathematics and public speaking needed to be included. The foundation of the Labour College represented the realisation of one of Maclean's most cherished dreams but it was overshadowed by more dramatic events. Maclean's arrest had followed almost immediately on from those of Willie Gallacher, John Muir and Walter Bell on charges arising out of the publication in the *Worker* of an article entitled 'Should the Workers Arm?' Although the substance of the article was a direct refutation of the proposition, the use of such an emotive title was sufficient to provoke the authorities to act.

The failure of Clyde workers to react in any effective way to the arrest of Gallacher and Muir may have encouraged the authorities to press home their advantage. They now steadfastly refused to make any concessions to the CWC, even refusing to meet a deputation, and towards the end of March they struck a decisive blow by arresting and deporting from Glasgow some of the CWC's leading figures. Kirkwood, Haggerty, Shields, Messer, and MacManus were removed from the scene and, with them gone, the militant wave ebbed away.[53] Some sporadic industrial action occurred but it remained patchy and was sustained only briefly. An attempt by MacDougall and Jimmy Maxton, the ILP'er friend of Maclean, to provoke a general strike against the deportations led only to their own arrests.[54]

The trials involving Maclean, Gallacher, Muir, Bell and finally Maxton, MacDougall and Jack Smith, the convener at Weir's factory, took place in Edinburgh in April and May 1916. Maclean appeared first to face six indictments including incitement to strike against conscription and an appeal to soldiers to lay down their arms. Although he placed on record his opposition to the war he denied the substance of the charges laid against him. This was a curious defence since he was clearly guilty of the offences in their essence. However, he genuinely believed that the specific charges were unwarranted in that he did not say or mean what was alleged against him by a procession of police officers. In effect he was arguing that there was a police conspiracy against him although his Counsel suggested that the charges could be explained in terms of misinterpretation by the police of what was actually said.

The jury took little time to decide on Maclean's guilt and the presiding judge, Lord Strathclyde, imposed an exemplary sentence of three years' penal servitude.[55] The severity of the sentence shook the other defendants and at their subsequent trial, Gallacher, Bell and Muir adopted a contrite attitude which was rewarded with sentences of twelve months each for Gallacher and Muir, and three months for Bell. The following month Maxton and MacDougall received twelve months while Smith was sentenced to eighteen months on account of his recalcitrant attitude in court.

Arguably no other aspect of Maclean's political career has provoked more speculation and controversy than the nature and effects of his periods of imprisonment during the war. Much of the controversy has centred on allegations that Maclean was ill-treated and specifically that his food was drugged. This allegation was initiated by Maclean's statement to the High Court at a subsequent trial in 1918 that his food had been deliberately drugged during his imprisonment in 1916-17. This was a charge which he repeated publicly after his release from prison at the end of the war. The belief that Maclean had indeed suffered dreadfully during his prison terms led Gallacher and others to speculate that his mental faculties had been so seriously impaired as to undermine his political balance.

Much of the debate about Maclean's mental and physical condition while in prison and the behaviour of the authorities to him has been obscured by official restrictions on access to relevant records. One scholar, Gerry Rubin, was allowed to see a selection of the available evidence which led him to discount Maclean's allegations of 'poisoning'.[56] We have subsequently seen what appears to be the complete official file dealing with Maclean. The fresh material supports Rubin, while offering some interesting observations and insights into the way authorities came to see Maclean.

The first point to bear in mind is the almost complete absence of precedent available to the Scottish Office in dealing with prisoners who were not criminals in the accepted sense. Secondly the ordinary prison authorities, and in particular the relevant medical practioners, had no initial knowledge of who Maclean was other than the obvious fact that he was a convicted felon. James Devon, Prison Commissioner of Health for Scotland, had once delivered a lecture to a co-operative audience and answered questions on the treatment of first offenders. Although Maclean and MacDougall attended the lecture and participated in the subsequent discussion this fleeting point of contact was apparently forgotten by all concerned.[57] But if Devon forgot his first meeting with Maclean, he was to become intimately concerned with his case during this and subsequent periods of imprisonment. Together with Dr Gilbert Garrey, Medical Officer at Peterhead Prison and Dr Hugh Ferguson Watson, Medical Superintendent of the Criminal Lunatic Department at Perth Prison, Devon was responsible for Maclean's medical supervision. They were involved in all Maclean's later imprisonments when the issue of his treatment was recognised as politically sensitive.

While the cases of the Clyde prisoners and deportees attracted press attention, Maclean's became the most celebrated, probably because of the relative severity of the sentence. Establishment newspapers like the *Glasgow Herald* saw this as entirely warranted to stamp out behaviour of a seditious, even treacherous, kind. But socialist newspapers saw the sentence as further evidence of growing State repression and the continued weakening of liberal principles and freedoms. Perhaps the most direct condemnation of the trial came in the somewhat unlikely columns of the *Cotton Factory Times*. There the trial was seen as a simple travesty of justice and the law as a tool of the State: 'The law is elastic; elastic enough to stretch over any person whom the authorities wish to put out of the way; and this is what has been done in the case of John Maclean.'[58]

His case was publicised by Mrs Bridges Adams, the progressive educationalist and tireless opponent of the war. She used the *Cotton Factory Times* to denounce the failure of Labour Parliamentarians to protest about the treatment of Maclean and the others on Clydeside. Her strongest criticism was reserved for Hyndman, the Countess of Warwick 'and their aristocratic ecclesiastical association in the Church of the Resurrection' who remained silent on the sufferings of their former political comrade.[59]

In practical terms the campaign mounted on behalf of Maclean had two elements. The first was the demand that he should be released. Maclean insisted that he would not plead for mitigation of his sentence but hoped that the BSP would organise action designed to force the authorities to grant his release. In July his wife wrote to Albert Inkpin, Secretary of the BSP, expressing Maclean's disappointment that no demonstrations or physical protests had been launched on his behalf. Inkpin replied that, since they were expressly forbidden by Maclean himself to submit any plea for clemency which involved an admission of guilt, there was little the BSP could do in practical terms beyond applying the conventional forms of pressure such as resolutions and getting sympathetic MPs and public figures to take up the case.[60] In fact the Scottish Office was virtually deluged with resolutions from socialist and labour organisations from all over Britain.[61] This was a pattern repeated on later occasions.

The second element involved the demand that while in prison Maclean should not be treated as an ordinary criminal but accorded political status. This demand was made in various resolutions submitted to the Scottish Office and by Maclean to the Secretary of State, Mackinnon-Wood, soon after the start of his prison term. The question of political status was discussed by officials, some of whom were minded to grant it in cases of those convicted of sedition. However, higher authority rejected such a course having rehearsed the arguments in the case of Walter Bell, and coming to the conclusion that so-called 'political prisoners' should be treated in the same way as other convicted felons.[62] The issue was one which continued to be raised, particularly when it was seen that imprisoned Sinn Feiners in Britain and Ireland were accorded a form of special category status. But while the Scottish Office turned its face against any official categorisation of 'special' or 'political' offender, it was accepted that the prison regime could be operated in a more flexible manner on occasion. Certainly Maclean's subsequent treatment in prison reflects a conscious, if informal, willingness to grant him privileges not normally available to convicts.

The possibility that Maclean might be granted parole or an early release, or both, and the subject of his prison status were not matters for the prison authorities or Scottish Office civil servants. They were ultimately matters of political calculation. However, demands for Maclean's release became increasingly framed in terms of his physical and mental health as rumours began to circulate that he was becoming ill. In May 1916, Mrs Bridges Adams published a letter from Agnes Maclean in the *Cotton Factory Times*. The letter was written shortly after a visit to her husband which alarmed Mrs Maclean. According to Mrs Maclean the treatment was

> most degrading and injurious to health. The feeding is very poor, about one hour is allowed for exercise daily, the rest of his time is filled up in doing prison work picking oakum. He is allowed to read . . . but no newspapers, no contact with the outside world at all. I do not know how he will stand that for so long. He is not allowed to write or see me for another seven months.[63]

Maclean was already making allegations that his food was being drugged, an accusation which suggested to the medical authorities that he was becoming mentally unbalanced. The root cause of Maclean's allegations of food drugging was very simple; the food was making him ill and he concluded that it must be doctored. The combination of prison food and illness became common enough and the CWC leader John Muir never recovered physically from its effects, which many held responsible for his early death. When Maclean intimated that his own illness was caused by food which had been deliberately adulterated, with the object of undermining his political effectiveness, it clearly confused the

99

doctors. They knew his food was not drugged and could think of no reason why a normal individual should think it could or would be drugged. Since they had no reason to think him special they thought Maclean's assertion of importance linked to the drug allegations meant he was someone with 'a peculiar mental twist'.[64]

Various representations, aimed at securing Maclean's early release, including a number from George Barnes, former leader of the ASE and currently a Labour MP, were rejected.[65] Instead, in early March 1917 Maclean was reported as having been moved to Perth for observation since he was showing signs of lack of mental balance. MacDougall had already been moved to Perth suffering from a nervous breakdown and the authorities were concerned to 'avoid giving anyone the chance of using the mental breakdown of Maclean and MacDougall as a basis for attacks on the Government or prison system'.[66]

In Perth, Dr Watson noted that Maclean continued to parade the delusions about drugging which began in Peterhead and these made him wary of taking medicine prescribed for the treatment of chronic catarrh. But having been put on a special diet his physical and mental condition improved and he began to take medication. Dr Devon, who had a long talk with Maclean in June, thought he looked ten years older than his true age and while he 'reasons quite clearly . . . it is evident that he has not got rid of his suspicions and of his insane delusions of persecution'.[67] Watson, although satisfied that Maclean's delusions had largely disappeared at Perth, nonetheless saw him as a 'highly strung, neurotic subject' who would never be 'an ordinary sane man again'.[68] Indeed Watson thought that Maclean's mental health actually benefited from the quiet conditions inherent in imprisonment which removed him from externally generated excitement such as appeared to follow the visits of his wife, described by Watson as 'awkward'.

The possibility that Maclean might be released early gained momentum within the prison system by June. By that stage only Maclean and Jack Smith, of the Clydeside prisoners, remained in jail and Smith was due to be released shortly. The prospect of an intensified campaign focused on the single, and singularly emotive, case of Maclean may have increased the attraction of resolving matters by releasing Smith and Maclean together. Indeed the decision to let them out of prison at the end of June was defended as 'an act of expediency only'.[69] It is possible that the actual timing of the release was prompted by the intervention of the Prime Minister's Office which raised the issue with the Scottish Office in mid-June.

Lloyd George had received a letter from George Lansbury appealing for clemency on humanitarian grounds. He observed that Maclean had many of the radical characteristics which Lloyd George would recognise in himself and urged him to secure Maclean's release. According to Lansbury, Maclean was suffering from delusions and becoming mentally unbalanced: 'His wife dreads his going mad'.[70] If Maclean was released Lansbury undertook to take him to the south coast of England where he could recuperate with his family in peace. It is not clear whether this appeal did more than simply emphasise the 'expediency' of letting Maclean go before some permanent damage was done to his health, with dangerous consequences for the government's reputation on Clydeside. In any event Maclean was released from prison on 30 June on a ticket-of-leave which required him to report to the police weekly.

He remained in Scotland for about a fortnight before leaving with his family for Hastings where Lansbury had arranged for him to stay at the Carlton Private Hotel.[71] Before travelling south Maclean wrote to the *Scottish Co-operator* to thank:

all co-operators and other friends that have congratulated me on my release . . . Not only had I to endure barbarous cruelty myself but I saw conscientious objectors who likewise are suffering in a similar manner . . . I might state that my doctor has assured me that I am only suffering from a slight nervous strain and a general catarrh, and that all I require is good food, fresh air and a rest.[72]

One potentially difficult situation which arose at this point was resolved by George Barnes who arranged for the cancellation of Maclean's army call-up papers following his release. Maclean was also granted permission to meet his obligation to report weekly by sending a letter stating his current whereabouts to the relevant police force. [73]

There is little doubt but that Maclean experienced a nervous breakdown during his imprisonment. Indeed such an experience was common enough amongst conscientious objectors and was shared by MacDougall and probably John Muir. We have seen that the prison medical authorities considered Maclean to be mentally unstable and indeed claimed that though he was kept in prison 'he was treated on the same basis as an insane man'.[74] It might be argued that this type of diagnosis was prompted by his extreme political views and his anti-social behaviour, in much the same way that dissidents were alleged to have suffered from mental disorder in the Soviet Union. Certainly there appears to be a tendency on the part of at least one doctor to label the likes of Maclean as mentally unbalanced on the grounds that 'he has such an exalted opinion of his own importance that he believes criminal efforts are being made to injure his usefulness'.[75] Jack Smith was also described as 'not very stable mentally' and Mac-Dougall was likewise seen as similarly demented. However, it is apparent that Maclean did appear unbalanced in his behaviour to his wife.

What is at issue, then, is not whether Maclean actually suffered a nervous breakdown but the nature and implication of that breakdown for the future. Was Maclean never going to be an ordinarily sane man again, or was the breakdown a temporary phenomenon brought on by the rigours of prison which would disappear once he was removed from that environment? We are obviously unqualified to make a judgement on something so difficult to evaluate as mental disorder, particularly from a distance of more than half a century. What we can say is, that according to the medical practitioners who dealt with Maclean during all his prison terms the only manifestation of 'delusion' or 'persecution mania' concerned his suspicion of prison food. The very specific character of Maclean's 'delusion' was literally underlined by one doctor in his notes [76] while another clearly thought that the refusal to eat prison food and to hunger strike was not a sign of mental illness. Thus when the question of certifying Maclean as insane was raised with Dr Gilbert Garrey, the doctor most immediately concerned with Maclean's medical condition, he refused to sign any such certificate and the issue appears to have been dropped. [77]

Certainly after Maclean had spent some time in Hastings his health visibly improved. According to police enquiries he spent most of his time relaxing on the promenade listening to the local bands. When a reporter from the *Call* came to interview Maclean he expected to find a shattered individual. Instead he found the reverse: 'What struck me most was the fierce intensity of his devotion to the cause of socialism. He is big and strong, energetic and capable looking.' [78] No doubt the overthrow of the Tsarist regime encouraged Maclean to believe that further, dramatic changes were imminent and that the social revolution in Europe was indeed a prospect.

At the end of July Maclean moved briefly to London, notifying the Metropolitan Police that he would be staying in Stratford. His purpose in coming there was to attend an abortive conference called to discuss the idea of setting up a British version of Workers' and Soldiers' Councils. It is likely that while in London he would have met members of the BSP Executive, probably Fairchild and Alexander, and in August he was introduced to Chicherin with whom he had a long talk a few days before the latter's internment.[79] He subsequently wrote to Chicherin expressing the view that Marxism was 'growing rapidly and with it the interest in, and importance of all connected with Russia, yourself included'.[80] But this letter and others to the Petroffs were withheld by the authorities.

When Maclean returned to Glasgow in the autumn of 1917 his main effort focused on the development of Marxist education and by early November he claimed to have 500 workers attending his Glasgow class every Sunday and a further 100 attending a class in Govan. Altogether he ran eight classes a week in Scotland with a membership of over 1,000 while MacDougall ran classes for a further 300 workers, mostly coal-miners.[81] As well as his educational work Maclean was instrumental in the formation of the Russian Political Refugees Defence Committee.

In this endeavour he was assisted by an emigré Russian shoemaker, Louis Shammes, and together they organised or 'engineered' the sending of resolutions protesting against the internment of Chicherin and the Petroffs. A letter sent to the *New Statesman* at the end of November and signed by Maclean and Shammes brought both to the attention of MI5.[82] But by then the news of a Bolshevik revolution in Russia had further emboldened Maclean and increased the tempo of his educational and propagandist activity. As Willie Gallacher recalled Maclean had become a 'driving dynamo of energy, driving, always driving towards his goal ... The work done by Maclean in the winter of 1917-18 has never been equalled by anyone. His educational work would have been sufficient for half a dozen ordinary men, but on top of this he was carrying on a truly terrific propaganda and agitational campaign'.[83] With the success of the Bolsheviks and the repatriation of Chicherin and the Petroffs to Russia in January 1918, Maclean's status as the outstanding revolutionary figure in Britain seemed assured.

The regard with which he was held by the Bolsheviks had been underlined by his adoption as an Honorary President of the Petrograd Soviet and his appointment as Soviet Consul in Glasgow on the instructions of Chicherin, who had succeeded Trotsky as Commissar for Foreign Affairs. This appointment caused consternation in the Foreign Office who did not know of Maclean but believed that the 'choice of the Clyde for the appointment of a Bolshevik Consul is significant'. When they contacted the Home Office for information on the individual concerned, the reply served to confirm their fears: 'If this record is as stated there would be amply sufficient grounds to object to his appointment. If he should be at liberty in Glasgow the police ought to watch him. They were assured that he was being watched'.[84]

Ironically the telegram concerning Maclean's appointment as Consul in Glasgow was initially received by Sir Donald Maclean, the leading Scottish Liberal politician. He contacted Ramsay MacDonald who relayed the telegram to the 'real' Maclean. In such a curious fashion did Maclean receive his formal notification of appointment. Armed with his credentials, Maclean set up his consulate at 12 South Portland Street, but the British authorities refused to recognise the 'so-called Soviet Consul' even to the extent of refusing to deliver mail addressed in that form.[85] This interference briefly led to a misunderstanding between Maclean and Litvinov, the Bolshevik representative in London, who each accused the other of not responding when letters were in fact being intercepted.

Maclean took his appointment seriously and in typical fashion now refused to meet his parole requirement of reporting weekly to the police. Until December he had complied by weekly letter; now he declared to the Secretary of State, 'it is meaningless in view of my public position as Russian Consul in Glasgow and is derogatory to the great Russian Republic'.[86] No action was taken by the Scottish Office but Maclean once more preoccupied the authorities, particularly as his propaganda became increasingly inflammatory. He publicly urged Scottish workers to follow the example of their Russian comrades, and as war-weariness set in it was feared that such a message would undermine the war effort. This was intensified with the initial success of the German offensive in early 1918 and Maclean now became subject to close, but fairly open surveillance by the Security Services. Shorthand reports of what he said were openly taken at his meetings but this overt intimidation did nothing to dampen the tenor of Maclean's revolutionary message.

In February the General Officer commanding the Army in Scotland outlined his fears about the situation in Glasgow 'where indications of unrest continually prevail'.[87] He wanted action taken against Maclean and suggested that if his parole could not be cancelled a renewed prosecution should be mounted. Another report on the role of agitators distinguished between those like MacManus, Gallacher and Maxton who keep to industrial issues and the even more notorious Maclean and MacDougall who continually raised political questions including the war. Particular concern was expressed about their influence on miners in the Fife coalfield.

Certainly the file on Maclean's activities in the period from late 1917 to spring 1918 is substantial but the belief that he should be arrested to prevent him influencing workers was not universally held. In the middle of March 1918 the Chief Investigation Officer of the Ministry of Munitions in Glasgow, Mr J. Matson, recorded his opposition to arrests. He believed that they were unnecessary and could make things worse. Matson argued that the industrial scene was calm and the influence of agitators was on the wane.[88] This was almost certainly a shrewd evaluation of the prevailing situation and, once the German offensive had been halted and reversed, demands for a negotiated end to the war lost most of the popular support which had seemed to be growing behind the anti-war agitation.

In a sense it was precisely because the industrial situation was so calm that a strong move against Maclean could be calculated to be effective. Such a move was virtually inevitable, given the openly seditious character of Maclean's propaganda which was unsurpassed by anyone else and represented a challenge to the government. As officials noted, if Maclean could get away with such statements then it would be impossible to prosecute anyone else. There was some concern in the Scottish Office as to whether Maclean possessed diplomatic immunity against arrest and the Foreign Office was consulted. They denied that he was a diplomat but wanted to be kept in touch with developments, observing that it was a delicate issue involving international policy.

In fact Maclean was arrested in April and tried in May on charges relating to sedition. The range and nature of the offences retailed in the indictment illustrated the extent to which Maclean had moved towards a new conception of revolution closer to Liebknecht and Luxemburg, and even Lenin, than to pre-war Second International notions. In conducting his own defence at the trial Maclean concentrated on turning the trial into an agitational–propagandist occasion with the condemnation of capitalism and the war as its central theme. In a speech lasting more than an hour Maclean made his oft-quoted remark, 'I come here not as the accused but as the accuser of capitalism dripping with blood from head to foot'.[89] As a result of his uncompromising revolutionary denunciation of the system Maclean was sentenced to five years in prison. The sentence was to be served, as before, at Peterhead prison.

As Tom Johnston observed, Maclean's sacrifice only made sense if it produced the desired effect on Clydeside workers. But while they might admire his courage and resolve, the overwhelming majority continued much as before.[90] There remained the possibility that the government might be influenced in its treatment of Maclean by the requirements of Anglo-Soviet policy. Lenin was clearly aware of Maclean's plight and in his concluding speech at the fourth Congress of Trade Unions declared that the British government imprisoned him 'because he exposed the objects of the war and spoke about the criminal nature of British Imperialism . . . and this time not only as a Scottish school-teacher but also as Consul of the Federative Soviet Republic'.[91] But following the conclusion of the Brest–Litovsk Treaty, which effectively ended Russia's participation in the war, the Soviets had no real diplomatic or other form of leverage to exercise on behalf of Maclean. So Maclean entered prison with every prospect of serving a long and debilitating sentence, but still determined to refuse to eat the prison food which he believed to be doctored. When he entered Peterhead prison the authorities attempted to defuse the situation by offering to allow food to be brought in to Maclean from outside the prison provided he agreed to accept prison food in the interim. Maclean initially agreed and was permitted to contact his wife to make the necessary arrangement. However, before she was able to reach Peterhead, Maclean had gone on hunger strike complaining that the prison food was making him unwell and demanding that he be transferred to prison in Glasgow.

The possibility of a prison transfer was also raised by Ramsay MacDonald in a letter to the Secretary of State, Robert Munro, in early July 1918, who pointed out the practical difficulties of arranging for food to be brought to the prison. No food was entering Peterhead at this stage and Maclean's hunger strike was broken by the decision to force-feed him. Dr Garrey was in charge of the physical process which began on 1 July and argued that a more realistic description of what took place was artificial feeding. He claimed that nothing which would ordinarily be described as physical violence took place and daily reports of Maclean's diet and condition were relayed to the Scottish Office. The issue became public following a routine visit to her husband in October by Agnes Maclean who described herself as shocked by his appearance. She told the authorities in Peterhead that he was 'worn and ill'. 'He is not in good health and it is no use trying to blind me to the fact that his health is rapidly being broken.'[92] In fact the question of Maclean's sanity was being discussed by Drs Devon and Watson with specialist advice being sought from Harley Street doctors. But, as indicated earlier, Dr Garrey, who was most immediately responsible for Maclean's medical treatment and the doctor with day to day access to him, was unwilling to sign the necessary certificate. Writing at the end of September 1918, Garrey concluded: 'Mentally he is quite clear and alert and does not show any sign of insanity but is evidently quite determined to pursue his present policy so far as feeding is concerned'.[93]

It is apparent that Maclean was likely to remain imprisoned at least until the end of the war, despite the growing number and volume of protests and representations being organised on his behalf. George Barnes, who was probably the most influential Labour figure still in the government at this stage, had made it clear that he would not press for Maclean's release while the war continued, though he was prepared to try to ameliorate the conditions of imprisonment.

In fact Maclean clearly was granted privileges with regard to the reading material made available to him in prison. He was denied access to contemporary newspapers and periodicals but the list of books he requested testified to the wide range of his interests. This encompassed the anticipated literature of political economy and history but included books on psychology and physics. It was made clear to Maclean that the abandonment of his hunger strike could lead to further relaxation in his prison regime but he resisted such blandishments and the process of forced, or artificial, feeding continued.[94]

In October 1918 the Gorbals Labour Party adopted Maclean as their Parliamentary candidate in preference to the sitting Labour MP, George Barnes. Maclean was eligible to become a Labour candidate since the BSP was an affiliated organisation but his selection caused Labour's National Executive Committee some embarrassment. The NEC was concerned to avoid the spectacle of Barnes being challenged in the Gorbals by an official Labour Party candidate who was currently in prison on a charge of sedition. Nevertheless Maclean was reluctantly endorsed and Willie Gallacher assumed the responsibility of organising the electoral campaign on his behalf.

Barnes had taken an interest in Maclean's case during the earlier period of imprisonment but in 1918 refused to use his position to secure Maclean's release as long as the war lasted. With the end of the war on 11 November, Barnes now urged that Maclean be released so that he could meet the electoral challenge of revolutionary socialism in the Gorbals. Maclean was notified on 16 November that he would be released shortly and was permitted to notify his wife in advance. He advised her that he hoped for a quiet return to Glasgow: 'My strongest desire is to get right home without anyone waiting for me at the station . . . remember absolutely no demonstrations in Glasgow that can be left till after.'[95] He was actually met by a large crowd of friends and supporters and was intoxicated by the reception. But from then on he remained largely out of public view, playing no active part in the electoral campaign until he appeared at an eve of poll rally. Indeed he never seems to have met his opponent during the whole campaign, although Barnes was willing to meet so 'interesting' a personality.

One curious aspect of Maclean's early release, which did owe much to Barnes's determination that he should be free for the election, was the subsequent decision of the Scottish Office to follow it up by supplying him with a Free Pardon. Maclean typically rejected the notion of a Free Pardon in contemptuous terms as well as issuing a demand for compensation,[96] but quite why the pardon should have been made in the first place has not previously been explained. In fact it was issued because it was feared by the Scottish Office that Maclean might well defeat Barnes and that, as a still convicted felon,he would be disqualified from taking his seat in Parliament with all the political pyrotechnics which would inevitably follow. To avoid such an eventuality the Free Pardon was granted and, as if to underline the instrumental rationale behind it, the Secretary of State specifically ordered that it be dated from the day Parliamentary nominations opened. [97]

If Maclean's 1918 Parliamentary campaign began in controversy it certainly ended in similar circumstances. As we have noted, Maclean's only real appearance during the election was at an eve of poll rally. According to the accounts of Tom Bell and Willie Gallacher, Maclean's performance disappointed and saddened an expectant audience. He apparently rambled in a disjointed manner, preoccupied with accounts of his prison experiences and particularly the attempts of the authorities to break him. This occasion is used by Bell and Gallacher as the clearest example of Maclean's mental degeneration which both emphasise as the cause of his later estrangement from the BSP and emerging CPGB.

Obviously at this distance in time, it is difficult to judge the mental state of someone who had spent a significant recent period of time in prison, latterly being artificially fed. We have tended to take the Bell–Gallacher account at face value as a reasonable description of Maclean's mental state at this time yet emphasise that once beyond the immediate post-prison period, and certainly from early 1919 onwards, further examples of obvious mental instability on Maclean's part are not forthcoming. However, a question mark can be placed against the Bell–Gallacher account of the pre-election meeting by juxtaposing the accounts carried in the *Scotsman* and the *Glasgow Herald*,[98] newspapers not noted for their support of Maclean's capacity for rational mental reasoning. Had Maclean's performance at the St Mungo Hall rally been as disastrous as Bell–Gallacher indicated, and especially had the audience been so disappointed in it, then both the newspapers would have trumpeted it loudly. Yet their accounts make no such allusion, and beyond observing that Gallacher introduced Maclean to the audience as someone who had suffered a nervous breakdown, their accounts of his performance were similar and fairly typical of a Maclean public speech before 'a crowded and enthusiastic meeting'. His speech was vigorous and straightforward: 'a gust of discursive oratory, slightly autobiographical, merely adumbrating his political principles and concentrating on his personal achievements . . . He was occasionally vituperative, delivering fluent denunciations of legal and medical scoundrels . . . The egotistical note was sounded throughout, a sense of humour was less apparent.'

Neither newspaper suggests that the audience reacted negatively to the speech, nor do they suggest that it was the performance of someone exhibiting the signs of mental delusion or disorder. Maclean was undoubtedly egotistical in the manner of most revolutionaries who have to sustain themselves out of their own sense of right and destiny. He had always emphasised the importance of honesty, integrity and a sense of personal political honour, and saw himself as possessing such qualities. His lack of ready or easy humour was well known to political allies as well as foes. But he was not egocentric and in emphasising his prison sufferings he always related them to the similar 'torture' being endured by conscientious objectors and Sinn Feiners and, later, political prisoners in the United States, notably Tom Mooney. He never, and certainly not at this rally, saw his prison experience as unique. In weighing the significance of the Bell–Gallacher account of Maclean's pre-election day speech it is worth remembering the accounts of the newspapers, who had no reason to underplay any signs of delusion or ignore any display of impatience or dismay on the part of the audience.

What may have alarmed and dismayed Gallacher was the general tone of Maclean's remarks which had little to do with winning votes, and indeed clearly asserted that the political significance of the general election was largely irrelevant, since developments were taking the class struggle on to a new and higher plane. Such deprecatory remarks about the value of election success must have stung Gallacher, whose own energetic efforts to gain Maclean's election were being so casually devalued. In the event Maclean was defeated by Barnes on the same kind of scale suffered by most Labour and ILP candidates on Clydeside. But it was the Gorbals figures which Lloyd George searched out and greeted with most obvious pleasure on the day the results were declared.[99]

5 'Poets, sentimentalists and deserters of the cause. . .'

The history of revolutionary socialism in Britain was dominated between May 1919 and January 1921 by the tortuous negotiations and efforts to establish a single unified Communist Party. One of the distorting effects of hindsight is to confer a sense of inevitability on events which actually took place and to create an impression of deviance or eccentricity on those who swam against the stream. The relationship between Maclean and the emerging Communist Party of Great Britain (CPGB) offers an example of this distortion. In 1918 the one British figure who might have been expected to play the leading role in such developments was the first Bolshevik Consul for Scotland. His opposition to the war and his response to the October Revolution had been clearly and unequivocally 'Leninist' in character; the same cannot be said of many of the figures who actually came to dominate and lead the emergent Communist Party.

The BSP of 1918 had finally seemed to be moving on a leftward trend in the direction pioneered by its intransigent Scottish campaigner. As we have observed, Maclean had been out of action for a short period in December 1918 recuperating from the stresses of imprisonment. But at the turn of the year he returned to the political fray with his usual indefatigable energy. His reputation and stature as a figure of unimpeachable Internationalist principle had spread around the world of revolutionary socialism in a manner equal to that of Liebknecht in Germany.

Domestically, Maclean emerged from relative isolation within the British Left and it is significant that for most of 1919 he campaigned in England rather than in Scotland as had been his usual pattern. Viewing events both at home and abroad in early 1919 Maclean believed that a revolutionary process was evolving in Britain which could be translated into a revolutionary fact by the determined action of a working class organised and aware of its historic mission. Maclean was hostile to a growing fashion amongst some of the revolutionary Left who believed that capitalism was now so weak that its demise was assured, that like an apple it would simply drop into the hands of the working class [1]. Rather, he continued to emphasise the vitality and strength of capitalism and its capacity to regenerate. The social revolution was only inevitable provided the working class was capable of knocking capitalism out and provided revolutionaries worked to convince the working class that it was capable of delivering such a blow. [2] Maclean's desire to participate in a final decisive struggle against British capitalism and his sense that such a struggle was almost at hand did not blind him to the need to analyse events closely. As we shall see, Maclean was not only the most consistent and persistent advocate of a revolutionary strategy in 1919 but the first British socialist to recognise that the revolutionary moment had passed and to urge a change in strategy. Whatever might be said of Maclean in this vital period, the accusation of ultra-leftism or revolutionary romanticism is decidedly inappropriate.

Maclean's activities in the early part of 1919 took him to Workington and Carlisle, back to Glasgow and onwards to London, where he received a tumultuous welcome from the BSP, before he turned north again to the textile and woollen industrial towns of Lancashire and West Yorkshire. [3] Maclean's progress on this tour was almost triumphal, with no evidence of mental instability. When he again spoke at St Mungo's Hall on 12 January, for the first time since the election, he was greeted by a packed meeting which was repeated the following night in Shettleston. An indication of Maclean's political presence can be gleaned from a report carried in the *Call* on 23 January: 'Maclean was in magnificent form and fully justified the contention of our members that he is pre-eminent as the standard bearer of Revolutionary-Socialism in this country . . . the audience at the end treated him to such an ovation that John must have felt his great sacrifices . . . have not been in vain.'[4] His message was the same; the class war was being fought out on an international scale and workers in Britain were obliged to play their part. If the Bolshevik Revolution was to be saved it could only be achieved by developing a revolution at home. Maclean interestingly came to this conclusion because he believed it would be more difficult to enforce a general strike on the apparently less radical objective of securing the withdrawal of British troops from Russia than one directed at full-blown social revolution. Maclean saw the need for revolution as urgent not only to defend Bolshevism in Russia but as the only way of averting a clash between Britain and America within the next five years. In the struggle for revolution Maclean saw the prime role being played by the coal-miners who were already locked into a potentially major strike over hours and conditions with the government under whose remit the industry came.

For Maclean the occasion of a national mining dispute offered the basis for a general strike built around the general demand for a drastic reduction in working hours throughout industry. Such a demand would draw the unemployed into the struggle and create a unity amongst workers which could be organised through workshop committees to effect control over the productive process. To that end Maclean urged workers to hold back until the miners struck and then to throw their weight behind that strike. To win, the miners required the pressure, 'not of one million coal miners but ten million workers . . . To achieve this it is not necessary to have the machinery of industrial unionism: all that is required is the class spirit and unity of demand'.[5] In this scheme of things the Forty Hours' dispute on Clydeside was premature but as Maclean noted, 'historical events never start and shape themselves as we plan them'.[6]

What Maclean could not easily forsee or easily combat was the skill with which a government directed by the supreme anti-socialist politician, Lloyd George, would handle the industrial challenge. In essence Lloyd George played a long hand against the miners offering a mixture of partial concessions and threats to keep the miners' leaders off balance and to spin the negotiating process out. Having agreed to set up a Royal Commission into the Coal Industry the government accepted its interim decision to increase wages and reduce hours and appeared to accept the principle of a nationalised coal industry. This interim or com-promise decision announced in March was seen by Maclean as a careful government trap designed to disarm the militant miners and obscure its own weakness. As Maclean observed, 'govern-ments never compromise unless they have to and now is the time to break up British capitalism for good'.[7] But the reality was that the government's strategy proved effective and was accepted by a majority of miners. Maclean's warnings were ignored or unheard. Certainly his hope that the rank and file would obey a call 'to stay out in defiance of their leaders' was utopian. In retrospect, Maclean would see this as the moment when the prospect for revolution passed, and while he still argued that capitalism is 'in the last ditch',[8] he became more pessimistic about the capacity of the working class to deliver the knock-out blow.

In October, during the railway strike, Maclean expressed his surprise and pleasure that the National Union of Railwaymen did not fold before the government's offensive. The unity shown by the railwaymen encouraged him but Maclean was no longer urging a general strike. Indeed he advised against it, since the 'impetus is on the side of the Government'.[9] A respite was now in order and this reflected his overall analysis of the changing balance of forces in society. His hope that this would be a pause in which workers would regroup and perfect their organisation gave way to the realisation that capitalism had regained the initiative.

While Maclean was seeking, throughout early 1919, to develop a revolutionary consciousness and confidence amongst industrial workers he was also participating in a struggle within the BSP over its revolutionary identity. E. C. Fairchild, who had assumed the party's leadership from Hyndman during the war, came to represent an anti-Bolshevik position. This manifested itself in terms of an explicit rejection of the Leninist conception of a soviet system of government, and the dictatorship of the proletariat. In essence, Fairchild was prepared to see Bolshevism as particular to the Russian experience but inappropriate to British circumstances.[10] At the Sheffield Conference held in April 1919 Fairchild articulated a political line which was derived from the perspective of a Second Internationalist. He emphasised the need to develop socialist unity and remain within the Labour Party and criticised the emergence of a new 'Third' International. Maclean attacked Fairchild and accused him of having gone over to the enemy. Instead of socialist unity Maclean demanded healthy activity, though he still spoke in favour of continued affiliation to the Labour Party. This latter issue was, for Maclean, less an issue of principle than a question of judgement. But above all Maclean rejected the cautious conception of a revolutionary transformation through the ballot box. In the current exceptional circumststances he urged: 'We must seize power and depend on the army and navy.'[11]

It would have seemed that the conflict within the party between a Left led by Maclean and a Right led by Fairchild and

Alexander was likely to resolve itself in victory for the former, expecially in view of the subsequent 'bolshevising' pressures on the BSP. In fact the triumph was neither to Fairchild nor Maclean. By 1921, the man eulogised by the *Call*, '(his) popularity in Scotland (is) rising like a flood tide . . . the principles of Revolutionary Socialism which Maclean stands for (are) captivating the minds of the workers',[12] had been marginalised: 'eased out', in his own words. The word 'marginalised' is not chosen casually. The developing debate as to the ideological character of a 'united' Bolshevik party in Britain was between the orthodoxy of the BSP with all its reformist overtones and an intransigent and sectarian ultra-leftism. Maclean was not the leader or supporter of the dominant orthodoxy; nor was he a protagonist of the minority tendency of 'super' revolutionaries, of implacable anti-Parliamentarianism. Yet this was the issue which formed the ideological content of the difficulties facing the participating organisations in the 'unity' negotiations. All the while Maclean remained on the sidelines to such an extent that militant BSP'ers in Glasgow itself, unhappy about their party's direction, were unaware for several months in 1920 that Maclean was outside the party.

Maclean's position reflected a more general paradox surrounding the character of the CPGB. The founding conference of the Communist International in March 1919 had invited delegates from five British bodies; the SLP; the IWW of England; The Industrial Workers of Great Britain; The Shop Stewards Movement; and, of the BSP, the 'tendency represented by Maclean'.[13] These bodies were conspicuous by their absence from the CPGB, finally launched in January 1921. The general historian's view that this party was a 'fusion of several small Marxist groups such as the British Socialist Party'[14] begs many important questions. A specialist version of the picture is even more misleading: 'If Marxist orthodoxy be defined as agreement with the ideas and practice of Russian Bolshevism then certainly the BSP was orthodox. Somewhat more eccentric and non-conformist was the Socialist Labour Party (SLP) the second largest organisation destined to lose its identity in the new Communist Party.'[15]

In fact, of the various groups involved in the attempts to create communist unity, only the BSP was to 'lose its identity' totally and permanently in the new party. Many groups and individuals remained outside, or like Sylvia Pankhurst and her associates, were rapidly expelled. 'Orthodoxy' is, of course, largely in the eye of the beholder, but the BSP had not previously been outstanding in its 'agreement with the ideas and practice of Russian Bolshevism'. Many would say that it was not afterwards either, if 'agreement' betokens something more substantial than an affirmation of faith. If the test were that of taking a revolutionary defeatist position on the war or that of offering the October Revolution 'a complete and unreserved blessing', those outside may well have passed better than those within.

The example of the Russian Revolution and the quickening domestic tempo might in themselves have provoked increased efforts towards unity amongst Britain's bickering revolutionary groups. The leftward drift of the BSP might have been enough to replace the vague aspiration towards 'socialist' unity by an urge to unify around a clearer set of revolutionary principles. This transition meant abandoning negotiations with the ILP, a process akin to swimming in thick soup; and negotiating instead with those bodies who would declare unequivocally for the Communist International, class war, dictatorship of the working class, Soviets or Workers' Councils, and the revolutionary overthrow of capitalism. All this might have happened. It is unlikely that without outside influence the issue would have been pressed to a conclusion within the period it was. The perseverance, the urgency, the direction, were supplied by the Russians either in the form of external directives and urgings or domestically through the agency of Theodore Rothstein.

It needs to be emphatically underlined that the BSP's 'orthodoxy' was what had previously been understood as Marxism. That 'orthodoxy' had none of the overtones of Leninism or Bolshevism which since 1917 have been inextricably entangled with that term. Moving from a social-democratic to a Leninist conception of Marxism and the road to social revolution was not simply a matter of degree or change of emphasis but a fundamental transformation of political outlook and understanding. Some, like Fairchild and Alexander, understood this but were unwilling to accept the change and therefore slipped out of the BSP. Others simply failed to realise the enormity of the ideological change and moved on into the CPGB without giving it much thought.

The new doctrines, then, received limited understanding in Western Europe and virtually none in Britain. Initial responses to the October Revolution seem to have been based on the premise that it was a confirmation of simple extreme postures and commended the stance of anti-Parliamentarians and opponents of reform. The earliest enthusiasts to do likewise, with the exception of Maclean and his faction of the BSP, came from this tendency. The London SLP and the near anarchist Glasgow Communist Group around Guy Aldred formed a short-lived Communist League in March 1919, and invited others to join on the principles of implacable denunciation of the ballot box and the idea that the struggle for working-class emancipation was 'a political struggle taking place on the industrial field'.[16] The Workers' Socialist Federation (WSF) with Sylvia Pankhurst, was slightly closer to Bolshevik reality and preferred to attend the first unity meeting in London on 13 May along with the BSP, SLP and South Wales Socialist Society (SWSS).[17]

Here the central problem was starkly displayed. To all the organisations, with the important exception of the BSP, the new revolutionary doctrine symbolised the rejection of Parliament in favour of soviets, revolution instead of reform. At least half the

BSP seemed to have no such commitment and even its left wing continued to favour running candidates for election, and, most damningly of all, supported affiliation to the Labour Party, home of careerists and social traitors. The BSP, of course, had recently been affiliated to the Labour Party after years of debate and had hardly grasped the new formula well enough to explain its commitments to Parliamentarism and Labour Party affiliation in revolutionary terms. The impasse resulting from these two questions was inevitable and appeared insoluble. Throughout the early period of the negotiations the WSF was scarcely resisting the temptation to call it all off and proclaim itself the Communist Party, while the SLP could barely disguise its suspicion of what it saw as the BSP's lack of revolutionary fire and principles.

In August correspondence from Lenin to Sylvia Pankhurst implied that these differences were of less significance than the need to create a Communist Party of any kind, or even, it was hinted, better that two Communist parties be created than none. The whole story of the preparation and launching of a British Communist Party has to be understood in this context of haste. The willingness to accept doctrines hardly understood and personnel who had no understanding at all is explained by the sense of urgency, first to catch a revolutionary tide and then later to rally all support for the protection of the Soviet Republic. It was a strategy with long-lasting consequences, not least of which was the estrangement of John Maclean. J. T. Murphy was later to reflect on these terms,

> Had the congress [2nd Congress of the 3rd International, July 1920, Moscow] examined the situation in each country and decided upon the formation of communist parties in those countries where the internal position of the working-class movement was ripe for such a decision; had it established itself as the revolutionary centre of the international working-class striving to create a single international through the internal conquest of the working-class move-

ment; it would not have thrust upon small immature groups of communists the tasks and responsibilities of independent parties and made it easy for the reactionaries to thrust them into isolation.[18]

The second half of 1919 and the start of 1920 were occupied by the respective parties to the proposed merger conducting referenda to discover the attitude of their members to the principle of unity and to the contentious features that went with it. Only the BSP, and that overwhelmingly, assented to all the required features, including affiliation to the Labour Party. The SLP's referendum affirmed unity and rejected affiliation whereupon the party dissolved its committee of delegates to the negotiations as their loyalty to the SLP position had become suspect. From this time Paul, McManus and Bell were acting unofficially as individuals. The WSF of course, rejected everything that unity would involve. Sylvia Pankhurst made her famous commitment to a direct and unswerving path to the revolution: 'The Communist Party must keep its doctrine pure, and its independence of Reformism inviolate; its mission is to lead the way, without stopping or turning, by the direct road to the Communist Revolution'.[19]

Meanwhile the position of the SLP had hardened and in March 1920 it asserted that it was now opposed to merger with the BSP. For a time the prospect of a 'left' Communist Party was seriously mooted: 'There must be no compromise with the B.S.P. Better a Communist Party without the B.S.P. than a party including the B.S.P. trailing with it the spirit of compromise to hamper the party in its revolutionary practice.'[20] Maclean had played no direct part in these controversies. His relationship with the BSP was unclouded during 1919; his articles in the *Call* were frequent and included reassertions of his commitment to the party. They also included important statements such as 'Will Capitalism collapse'? and 'Burn Bradbury and down with prices'.[22] The agitational and propaganda activities which preoccupied Maclean during this period were his efforts with the miners and his support for the 'Hands off Russia' campaign, at whose rallies he was the chief speaker. It was this latter which provided the occasion for Maclean's exclusion from the BSP and hence from the Communist Party of Great Britain. He attended his last executive committee meeting of the BSP in February 1920 and was excluded from its annual conference in April.

This rift was subsequently to be all but submerged in personal polemics and recrimination, but the issues ran deep, in some cases deeper than the protagonists may have realised. The unity negotiations were all-absorbing and the priority of party creation wholly appropriated whatever strategic and tactical thinking the BSP possessed. Maclean was not alone in lamenting the vacuum in BSP thinking on industrial and political strategy. His efforts in 1919 based on the development of militant and potentially revolutionary industrial activity had been applauded but not shared by the BSP. When, by the end of 1919, Maclean's own strategy appeared to be foundering on the rocks of capitalist restabilisation, the BSP had no other nor seemed to be participating in the debate. According to Harry McShane: 'he [Maclean] objected to their lack of an industrial and political perspective for Britain: "Hands off Russia" was the only policy they had.'[23]

This conflict in priorities seems to have come to a head in a discussion between Maclean and Theodore Rothstein. The latter, with Russian money at his disposal, offered Maclean a full-time paid post at the head of the 'Hands off Russia' campaign in which he had already figured so prominently. It appears that Maclean reacted violently both to the consequence that he would have to abandon his general educational and propaganda agitation and to what he regarded as Rothstein's effort to 'buy' him. This sentiment was interestingly shared in another context by J. Walton-Newbold: 'Rothstein had professed himself desirous I should become the Secretary of the "Hands of Russia Committee" but, no more than I would consider the editorship of *The Call* would I put myself in this position of dependence on the BSP and himself.'[24]

Gallacher tells us that it was after this disastrous encounter that Rothstein was informed of Maclean's alleged 'psychological disturbances'.[25] This information may have accounted for Rothstein's abrupt abandonment of Maclean and the setting in motion of the train of events which was to exclude from the BSP, and later the infant Communist Party, the one section which came closest to a Bolshevik way of thinking. Ernie Cant, described by Maclean as 'the cockney Cant', was dispatched to Glasgow to reorganise the BSP there. Maclean's Pollokshaws Branch was 'reorganised' out of existence and with it went his credentials as a delegate to the BSP's conference.

The extremity of Maclean's reaction to the meeting also requires explanation and a clue to this may be discovered in the circumstances of Rothstein's background. Russian by birth, he had arrived in Britain as a very young man around 1880 and was a long-standing member of the SDF/BSP. A 'leftist' in BSP terms, Rothstein's commitment to Bolshevism was equivocal before October 1917. He had been criticised by Lenin for advocating a defencist position on the war[26] and had in turn been a strong critic of Bolshevik undermining of the Kerensky government following the February/March revolution.[27] On the outbreak of war he appears to have resigned from the BSP in order to avoid arrest and possible deportation, though he continued to write for the *Call* under the pen-name, John Bryan, and played his part alongside Fineberg and Maclean in the defeat of Hyndman's patriotic faction.

It was during the course of the war that Rothstein's ability to combine paradoxical roles and associations was most enigmatic. Improbably, he obtained employment as a translator at the War

Office, and is even described by Sylvia Pankhurst as a confidential advisor to Lord Robert Cecil. The peculiarity of his positions is encapsulated by Walton-Newbold, 'He was a translator and interpreter at the War Office. He was the secret agent of Nicolai Lenin for the guidance of the Marxists of Great Britain and he was the Foreign Editor of the Daily News'.[28] The second role in this catalogue was expanded by inheritance from Litvinov, deported in September 1918 following the withdrawl of tacit recognition by the British government. The ambiguity of Rothstein's position could not be better illustrated than in this incident.

> Rex Leeper and Fedor Rothstein, a War Office translator, who later became Russian Minister to Teheran, arranged a meeting between Lockhart and Litvinoff . . . From the beginning of the meeting in a Lyon's restaurant in the Strand, Lockhart, Leeper and Rothstein made it clear that Soviet Russia would not be recognized.[29]

Bruce Lockhart, in his own memoirs, says that Leeper, a British diplomat of Australian origin who was for many years after 1917 the leading British expert on communist affairs, 'was on friendly terms with Rothstein . . . who . . . was an intellectual arm-chair revolutionary'.[30] In this way Rothstein, who 'had not at all the stand-point of Litvinov',[31] became 'the intermediary for subsidies to the revolutionary organisations and his secret activities were far reaching'.[32]

Whatever may be implied from this[33] Maclean cannot but have reflected on the contrast between Rothstein's war experiences and those of that other Russian refugee, his close collaborator Petroff;[34] not to mention Maclean's own privations. The disaffection he may have felt for Rothstein was no doubt accentuated by their lack of mutual contact. They do not seem to have known each other personally despite their shared experience of SDF, SDP and BSP membership. It was certainly augmented by some of the adherents being recruited by the BSP; among whom were

Lieutenant-Colonel C. J. Malone and, later, Francis Meynell, both of whom leapt to prominence in the BSP/CPGB during 1920. The former was a Coalition Liberal MP who had been on the Executive Committee of the anti-socialist and anti-Soviet Reconstruction Society. Following a visit to the Soviet Union Malone had been converted to a sympathetic view of the Bolsheviks and was speaking at 'Hands off Russia' rallies early in 1920. He was subsequently elected to the Provisional Executive Committee of the CPGB at the Unity Convention in July/August.[35] After speaking alongside Malone at a rally in Glasgow, Maclean refused to repeat the experience at a further rally in London. This was a breach of party discipline as well as a studied insult to the new recruit. Maclean's language was unambiguous:

> Since I spoke with him in St Andrew's Hall, Glasgow I have denounced him as an agent of the Government soothing the socialists whilst the Government was preparing for a Spring offensive against Russia.[36]

> To ask me to work with Malone for revolution is a joke. A man like that ought not to be allowed in a revolutionary Marxian party . . . To allow a Malone to lead a revolutionary party after a record such as his is high treason to communism. You might as well appoint Churchill as 'honorary' president of the Russian republic![37]

There is, in fact, no genuine evidence for the most extreme allegations against Malone. The accusation is mentioned by Saville and Martin, only to be dismissed as 'highly improbable'.[38] The less extreme criticisms are largely substantiated.

Maclean was not the only critic of Malone's Marxism. In a letter to Gallacher McGovern was also to comment, 'Remember that Colonel Malone's Communism has not kept him from supporting, in the Westminster (gas) House, a strong Air Force in defence of Imperialism . . . Turn out Sylvia Pankhurst for being too extreme and having some independence but keep the Khaki-clad colonels in your ranks'.[39] Klugmann points out that Malone received six months imprisonment for sedition following a speech in the Albert Hall on 7 November 1920, but also acknowledged his limitations, 'he had come over to the Party on an emotional rather than a reasoning basis; he was never a Marxist, and had little or no contact with the working-class movement. And, after his release from prison, he began to fall away from Party activity, leaving it before the General Election of 1922.'[40]

An even more disastrous appointment was that of Francis (later Sir Francis) Meynell, an appalling *poseur*, whose only claim to a background in communist politics had been his role as an intermediary in the scandal concerning the attempted transfer of Russian diamonds to the *Daily Herald*.[41] It was largely Meynell's great repute as a typographical expert which earned him his short-lived appointment as editor of the CPGB's weekly, the *Communist*, in place of Fred Willis, ex-editor of the *Call*. Maclean, in a deliberate echo of the wartime *Justice* exposé of Petroff, asked, 'Who is Meynell and what is Meynell are very appropriate questions. To my knowledge he was never in the SDF or the BSP. He has as much standing in revolutionary circles as Malone'.[42] The criticism of Meynell's leading role is substantiated by Meynell himself, who delighted in recalling that McManus, in offering him the editorship, 'did not mind in the least that I knew no Communist dogma, had read no Marx or Engels and had never heard of dialectical materialism . . . I doubt whether there could ever have been a political party organ that showed so little awareness of its party's ideology.'[43] When it was rumoured that the newspaper's editor would be charged with sedition in the spring of 1921, over its reaction to the failure of the Triple Alliance, Meynell hastily resigned his position and, in his own words, asked 'my father to make it plain to authority in the person of Sir Basil Thomson that I had already resigned my post'. Thomson already knew.[44]

The Communist Party used Maclean's suspicions of these leading figures as evidence of his mental instability but the conflict
ran deeper than a clash of personalities. It arose from the duality
of Rothstein's position in the politics of the extreme Left. He
was not merely acting as the crucial link between Russian and
British revolutionaries; he was effectively the representative in
Britain of the infant Soviet government. In this sense Rothstein's
loyalties were divided between a commitment to the International
(and British) revolution and his commitment to the needs of the
beleaguered regime. The overriding preoccupation with 'Hands
off Russia' stemmed from the second priority, though the possibility of a conflict between the two was not clearly identified by
anyone.

'Hands off Russia' was essentially an urgent attempt to build
a popular front-type movement with the single aim of campaigning for an end to external intervention in Russia. It was effective
because while most socialists in Britain neither understood nor
aimed to emulate the Bolshevik experiment, there was considerable sympathy for the Russians conducting their own affairs in
their own circumstances. Consequently Rothstein was appealing
to a wide variety of well-known public figures without wishing
to investigate their revolutionary credentials. The inclusion of a
figure like Malone, with his background as a Liberal MP and
formerly anti-Bolshevik campaigner, was seen as an important
capture by Rothstein but not by Maclean, who was applying
different criteria. The affair offers interesting anticipations of a
debate which became acute with the evolution of the 'Socialism
in One Country' doctrine nearly a decade later.

Maclean's position was unequivocally internationalist and
demanded that the BSP's energies be devoted to spreading the
revolutionary message in Britain. A British revolution was the
best service which could be offered to the Soviet regime whose
own prescription was still that the revolution in Russia could

only be sustained in the context of a general European revolution. In this strategy a 'front' campaign like 'Hands off Russia' was an important but partial element and then only when based firmly on working-class organisations. For Rothstein, Maclean's refusal to accept a paid, full-time role was evidence of disloyalty and political instability. It is important to recognise that Maclean was not objecting to Bolshevik 'interference' or using the familiar argument that 'Russian' methods were inapplicable to the British case. His loyalty to his own understanding of the principles of the Comintern was unwavering. James Hinton, in a critical passage, pointed out that

> Maclean's hostility to the Communist Party of Great Britain owed less to any far-sighted appreciation of the dangers of Russian domin- ation, than to the fact that it was London and Gallacher, rather than Maclean, who had Lenin's ear. It was not as agents of Moscow but as agents of the British Government that Maclean pilloried the leaders of the CPGB.[45]

In reality Maclean objected to the fact that Lenin's interventions were based on inadequate information on the changing situation of the revolutionary movement in Britain. And the inadequacy of that information was laid squarely at the door of British revolutionaries like Gallacher and Bell, who were presenting an absurdly inflated view of the British situation to the leaders of the Comintern.

By May 1920 the breach with the BSP was complete and made public by Maclean's starting again to publish the *Vanguard*. 'Dis- satisfaction with the plight of the BSP . . . has compelled us to resurrect the *Vanguard*'. The existence of the *Call* had made this unnecessary until the government 'paralysed the B.S.P. and the S.L.P.'[46] The first issue raised a further difference with the BSP which was to become a defining distinction in later quarrels with the CPGB. Maclean contrasted the BSP's endemic 'reformism', which he defined as an attachment to reform for its own sake, with the pursuit of reform as an instrument to create revolution: 'ours is the duty to formulate an immediate programme that will appeal to all workers and so prepare them for united action. We must have such a programme that no capitalist government will concede'[47]

Maclean described his own projected demands, which included a six-hour maximum working day, rationing work to absorb unemployment, minimum wages, price cuts and full maintenance for anyone still unemployed as a 'fighting programme'. It was basically the same kind of strategy which Maclean had been promoting since early 1919, when still an active member of the BSP, and anticipated the definition later elaborated by Trotsky as 'transitional demands'. It had nothing to do with the positions, attacked by Lenin in *Left Wing Communism*, which were the obstacles to the BSP's unity efforts directed at the other revolutionary organisations. Maclean needed no lectures from Lenin on ultra-leftism or infantile disorders.

Those who were in such need were being placed under enormous pressure in the period leading to the London Unity Convention, from 31 July to 1 August 1920, which formally proclaimed the CPGB. It was not Maclean or his strictures who were the main problem for the architects of a British Communist Party. They could be, and were, dismissed as the ramblings of an eccentric. The major obstacle was anti-Parliamentarianism and anti-Labour Party affiliation coming from the WSF, the SLP and the shop stewards. In this conflict between reformism and ultra-leftism Maclean was marginalised. Informed, no doubt, by advice from Rothstein, Lenin moved, with *Left Wing Communism* and the resolutions of the Second Congress of the Comintern, to harder positions against the ultra-left. Pankhurst and Gallacher in particular were persuaded by a combination of correspondence and personal contact to give the BSP its chance. The first victory was to create a split in the SLP whereby Paul, McManus and Bell created Communist Unity Groups. These, together with the BSP and a smattering of independent socialist groups, constituted the CPGB created at the London Unity Convention. The campaign was then to complete the unification process by bringing in the WSF which had, on 19 June 1920, declared itself and a small fringe of supporters to be the Communist Party (British Section of the Third International) (CP[BSTI]).

Maclean regarded these events with growing distaste and was himself engaged in a propaganda campaign in Scotland with a group of friends whom he labelled the 'Tramps Trust Unlimited'. This included his long-time collaborator, James Macdougall, Alexander (Sandy) Ross, ex-ILP and briefly ex-Glasgow police-man,[48] Peter Marshall, recommended by Ross, a conscientious objector and later a tutor at the Scottish Labour College, and Harry McShane, an engineer who had moved through the ILP and the Glasgow BSP. These five maintained a phenomenal output of leaflets, public meetings and literature sales. They were heavily involved in defending the cause of the Irish Republicans[49] as exemplified by their publication of the pamphlet, *The Irish Tragedy: Scotland's Disgrace* (June 1920). This activity contrasted sharply with the paralysis of the BSP, preoccupied with the unity negotiations.

The one area where the prospects for the CPGB were slimmest was Scotland. Here the BSP had always been a minority organisation among the revolutionaries to whom Parliamentary politics and affiliation to the Labour Party were anathema. Although Maclean was personally unaffected by this ultra-leftist disorder he believed it provided the opportunity for creating an alternative to the CPGB. Opposition to the reformism and opportunism of the BSP-sponsored grouping made common ground between Maclean, the SLP, and the Scottish Shop Stewards, including Gallacher and J. R. Campbell. These bodies met and constituted themselves as a Communist Labour Party (CLP) on 11 September 1920. Further discussion on the position of this embryo Communist Party for Scotland was postponed to a second conference on 2 October with J. R. Campbell in the Chair.

Meanwhile Gallacher, amongst others, had attended the Second Congress of the Comintern at which the full weight of the Russians had been thrown behind the BSP line on Parliament and Labour Party affiliation. Gallacher had been personally catechised by Lenin and obliged to recant his previous syndicalism and ultra-leftism. All this was unknown in Britain when Gallacher returned in time to intervene at the CLP meeting in October. He managed to persuade the delegates that they should, as the established CLP, apply to join the CPGB in which their voice would be crucial in reversing the BSP position on the two contentious issues. Maclean was outraged at Gallacher's hypocrisy in using his reputation as an anti-Parliamentarian in this way when he had actually abandoned his position and knew it had no chance within the CPGB in any case. This 'shameful bewilderment of the best fighting elements in Scotland'[50] ensured that the CPGB would now emerge as 'the Communist Party'.

Maclean believed that the type of dishonesty illustrated here was characteristic of the CPGB. He was later to claim that the party had attempted to deceive the casual observer into thinking he was a member by appointing a namesake as secretary of the CLP.[51] Again this claim could be used as evidence of Maclean's paranoia, but it is interesting that when *Communist* listed the names of the Executive the other John Maclean (of Bridgeton) appeared first, and his was the only name where the forename was given in full rather than simply by initials.[52] On 29-30 January 1921 the last act was completed when the CLP and the CP(BSTI) were brought into the CPGB fold at the Leeds Convention. 'All groups of British Marxists of any influence apart from the Left-Wing Group still working within the I.L.P. had merged their identity into a single united Communist Party of Great Britain.'[53]

The reality may have been slightly less triumphal. Four Manchester branches of the CP(BSTI) seceded rather than amalgamate and Sylvia Pankhurst's association with the CPGB was short-lived. In Scotland the SLP continued to provide an alternative forum, though Communist Party loyalists were anxious to decry its strength. Tommy Jackson claimed, 'We took out of the S.L.P. and into the C.P. every branch it had, bar three, and these we so depleted that two of them dissolved within a month or two'.[54] Maclean's objections to the new party were not just the obvious references to its theoretical poverty and immaturity, pertinent though these were. The BSP had accepted the formulae enunciated by Lenin in *Left-Wing Communism* and elsewhere because they seemed to correspond to beliefs they had always held on totally different premises and completely without the spirit of revolutionary intransigence which characterised Bolshevism. The Ultra-Left were bullied and pressured into accepting the same formulae in a hurry and their conversion was in many cases skin deep.[55] Deep-rooted syndicalist notions from time to time obliterated the core of political strategy. James Hinton comments that, 'it is very doubtful whether, by the time of the formation of the Communist Party in 1920-21, any substantial proportion of its members or leaders had grasped the Bolshevik idea of the party or would have approved of it had they done so'.[56] A contemporary observer made a similar assertion: 'Even in my immature mind it became clear that many professed members of the Communist Party had not earned their admission by faith and service. They were admitted into the party just as I had believed in my childhood that entrance into Heaven was assured by a solemn declaration of faith in God'.[57]

Deficiencies were unavoidable, but Maclean clearly believed that the haste, the methods of recruitment, and the speed with which converts were welcomed and translated into leadership

positions were making matters worse. The methods of recruitment also included liberal use of Russian gold. There was little
secret over this and the *Call* had always refreshingly argued that
the BSP ought to get its share of any of the fruits of international
solidarity. Maclean, too, had no objections in principle. When
he complained that the 'Communist Party has sold itself to Moscow with disastrous results both to the Russian and to the British
Revolutionary Movement' it was to the 'disastrous results' that
he addressed himself. An executive report from the SLP in 1920
had commented:

> The NEC wish to draw the attention of branches and the members
> generally to the most pregnant fact that the would-be disrupters
> of the revolutionary movement in this country are being subsidised,
> and subsidised parties are bound to attract more shades of opinion
> than there are colours in the rainbow, with what results the average
> S.L.P.'er can readily realise.

The result, according to Maclean, was a party composed of 'a
heterogeneous mixture of anarchists, sentimentalists, syndicalists,
with a sprinkling of Marxists'.[58] By contrast, men of principle
like Maclean (and he included his opponent, Fairchild, in this)
had been antagonised by Rothstein's efforts to 'buy' them and
had been 'slipped out' in consequence. A party which, in any
circumstances, would have had problems in terms of experience
and theoretical calibre had been flooded by 'Johnny-come-latelys'
for whom Maclean had only scorn and derision. Not just Malone
and Meynell, but the many others like Gallacher who had under-
gone late conversions were regarded with distrust. The ex-pro-
tegé of Maclean's was derided as a 'communist clown'.[59] He
'never was a marxian but an openly avowed anarchist' He had
'been to Russia and poses as the gramophone of Lenin'. It all
seemed the reverse of the proper process. 'A real revolutionary
party can only be established here based on Marx, not on Bakunin,

by fully avowed marxists of long years of standing.'[60] Maclean's problem, and perhaps Rothstein's, was that there were precious few of such description.

The way in which Maclean could be 'slipped out' with such ease has to be a reflection on his organisational capacities. His talents as a propagandist and agitator were never extended to the field of organisation. The opportunity existed throughout 1920. Harry McShane points out that his own South Side Branch of the Glasgow BSP was progessively disillusioned with the political and industrial indecision of the BSP nationally, and finally broke away in January 1920.[61] Yet McShane did not know of Maclean's break except by meeting him accidentally at Glasgow's May Day demonstration where Maclean was selling the revived *Vanguard*. No contact had been made with McShane's branch or its forty members. The SLP groups, the disaffected BSP'ers, the Gallacher–J. R. Campbell 'Worker' group and countless smaller bodies were only rallied to constitute the CLP on 11 September, well after the CPGB's founding conference, and more at the initiative of the 'Worker' group than of Maclean.

This deficiency may have been cause or consequence of a significant gap in the armour of Maclean's 'Bolshevik' theory. He had no grasp of the key concept of 'party'. The need for a party as provider of leadership, discipline, direction and a focus for disputed strategy or theory is entirely absent from Maclean's output. It should be said, of course, that the Bolshevik concept of the party was entirely foreign and totally uncomprehended by his British contemporaries and opponents as well.

For Maclean it was always enough for his friends or allies to be 'honest marxians'. His political associations were dictated much more by a sense of integrity or sincerity than by party loyalty or even shared ideological premises. His respect and admiration for Smillie is derived from this trait. Continuing relations with the SLP and individual members transcended the fiercest ideological clashes and the rivalry of separate party organisations. The style is exemplified in one of his letters to the SLP'er James Clunie: 'Your men, if in Glasgow, must come right up and identify themselves with us at meetings, and we'll here be only too pleased to put them upon the "stool".'[62] The same letters offer evidence of friendly co-operation with the Irish Communist Party, amongst others. Indeed, on occasion, Maclean seems to share Guy Aldred's sense of resentment at the CPGB's introduction of 'sectarianism', disrupting the solidarity and free exchanges between different groups on the revolutionary Left.[63] This kind of relationship needs to be set against one of the considered verdicts on his political alliances: 'The political effects of Maclean's paranoia . . . has hastened the rift with Gallacher; it blunted the edge of his propaganda speeches; and it increased the instability of his political associations.'[64]

In fact paranoia may have had less to do with Maclean's isolation than what David Howell has called 'the brittleness' of his 'organisational resources'.[65] Many of his 'political associations' were remarkably stable and durable. Where they were not, as in the case of Harry McShane, it was the result of the CPGB's organisational superiority and its legitimacy as the British heir of the revolutionary tradition. The Tramps Trust 'had conducted the best propaganda and agitation in the West of Scotland' but 'had left no organisation behind.'[66] The Communist Party and the Labour Party were removing the political space available to others. The part played by Maclean's temperament in embittering such ruptures may also have been a factor in squandering the political capital he once possessed within the international communist movement. After all, Maclean had once been the Russians' leading light in Britain and as late as May 1920 was being held up as the example for revolutionaries.[67]

Throughout the breach with the BSP Maclean believed that Lenin and the International were being systematically misinformed about the British situation. Part of this misinformation was that Maclean's strictures were the product of mental stress brought on by imprisonment. According to Gallacher, Lenin claimed that the Russians had a deal of experience of such problems and urged that Maclean visit the Soviet Republic, where he might receive any necessary treatment. Certainly Maclean would have been able to make his argument about the Rothstein/BSP strategy and recruitment policy. Other British socialists were visiting Russia; some from the Labour Party and the BSP were doing so legally with permits, others illegally and by clandestine means. Maclean, as so often, chose to make an agitational and propaganda issue out of the Foreign Office's arbitrary discretion in issuing permits to some and refusing them to others, including him. Maclean wrote a series of letters demanding permission to visit legally and these were reprinted in the *Vanguard*, together with exhortations to trade unionists to raise the question through their organisations. In practice the refusal to travel illegally meant forgoing the opportunity to acquaint the Comintern personally with his version of events. It was all very well to lament, 'Let Lenin realise that we are the real leaders of Communism and not the men who have got through to Russia'[68] but difficult to see how such realisation might have come about without personal contact.

Maclean's own answer was that the Comintern should take its information on Britain from his old collaborator, Petroff.

> In Russia, take your advice from neither Quelch nor Fineberg. Take it from Peter Petroff. Petroff is the only Russian who knows the working-class movement intimately in London and Glasgow [and] . . . is the only marxist in Russia that has any real comprehension of the situation here, and can fully explain this letter to you.[69]

Unhappily Petroff had not been in Britain since and may in any case have been preoccupied by his work in the Soviet foreign ministry. His presence in Britain might have served more purpose in offsetting Maclean's isolation in 1920 but his attempt to return here in February 1918 had been vetoed by the Home Secretary, Sir George Cave. The refusal was on the not unlikely grounds that Petroff 'now proposes to come as an emissary to the proletariat, that is to foment strikes and revolution'.[70] Like the expulsion of Litvinov, this was bad luck for Maclean and a considerable boost to Rothstein.

Maclean's differences with the CPGB, then, are no more to be dismissed as a product of nationalism any more than of mental disorder or of ultra-leftism. Unlike Pankhurst and many other early dissidents he showed greater tactical flexibility than Communist Party loyalists on several occasions. This was only to be expected in that Maclean, more than any of his domestic contemporaries, had developed, independently, Bolshevik ideas that they were busy learning as inflexible formulae. It was this understanding that made him acutely aware of the ideological deficiencies of the leading members of the infant Communist Party. Even at this point it is not clear that, as the matter is often stated, Maclean refused to join the CPGB. It is at least as sensible to state that he was excluded by the type of bureaucratic manoeuvre that was to become the hallmark of important elements within the Communist Party.

It is less important to establish 'blame' for the estrangement than to show that Maclean's arguments remained within a Marxist–Leninist frame of reference and involved no departure from Bolshevik principles. Even his 'nationalism' is grounded in a clearer international perspective than that possessed by many of his opponents. It has already been noted that these differences anticipate some of the major questions which confronted the Third International. The breach with Rothstein contains, in embryo, the issue of subordination of the needs of world revolution to the diplomatic requirements of the Soviet Union as well as the nature of united front tactics and the role of a Communist Party within them.

It is the distorting mirror of hindsight and the sheer longevity and durability of the CPGB which inclines one to examine the eccentricities of the dissident rather than the party. David Howell has observed that 'the international credentials of the Communist Party provided some defence against repeated disappointments and helped to ensure the continued adherence of a significant number of working-class activists'.[71] The matter was not only of 'credentials' but importantly, as J. T. Murphy observed, of money: 'had the Communist Party not received big financial shots in the arm, it would have been reduced and have probably gone out of existence within a year or two of formation, just as Sylvia Pankhurst's organisation and its paper died when they got no money from external sources'.[72]

Maclean plainly shared the SLP view that a party unable to sustain itself financially from its own working-class constituency had no political future. It was, as Murphy came to recognise, a wrong view. Maclean's breach with the BSP/CPGB came at the moment when mass unemployment began. To the brittleness of his organisational resources were now added financial problems. In contrast the CPGB, with sixty per cent of its small membrship unemployed, was still capable of maintaining a solid organisational structure, with a newspaper and an output of political pamphlets. It was at such a moment and for decades to come that even small financial shots in the arm were to be life-giving for the CPGB.

In retrospect the creation of the CPGB in 1920-21 with Russian goodwill and support was a decisive turning point in the development of the revolutionary movement. It reshaped the landscape of socialist politics outside the Labour Party and all those excluded from it or who chose to remain outside it were rapidly obscured from view. At the time such an outcome did not appear so obvious or inevitable and small groups of revolutionaries continued to operate. Maclean continued much as he had done during the war, when he was alienated from the Hyndman-dominated BSP.

6 *On the fringe*

At the time of the London Unity Convention a new issue had emerged in Scotland, that of the crofters in the Western Isles and their conflict with Lord Leverhulme. The modernisation programme of the Lewis and Harris Development Company Ltd faced many crofters with eviction. The Tramps Trust took the side of the squatters with enthusiasm. Ross went to Stornoway in July and Maclean followed on his return from Ireland. This was not without controversy among socialists and the SLP regarded it as a stand for the past and against the future, claiming that the crofters had as little to do with the British working class as Red Indian tribes has to do with the American. I. S. McLean, who has described Maclean's monetarist economic theories as 'oddly incongruous', also regards this involvement as idiosyncratic.[1] It is true that the argument was connected to an older conception of 'Celtic Communism' and a picture of communal peasant institutions which some have seen as parallelling the Russian *mir*. But in the case of the Russian *mir* that institution's potential as a 'starting point for a communist development' had been aired by Marx and Engels in their preface to the 1882 Russian edition of *The Communist Manifesto*. In Scotland Maclean may have seen the potential for a similar type of alliance between revolutionary socialism and agrarian radicalism, derived perhaps from his recent preoccupations with Ireland. Typically for Maclean the question had a distinctive, modern and international perspective, not generally shared by the many socialists who took up the crofters' cause that summer. He claimed that Leverhulme was 'preparing Lewis and Harris for the navy in case of war with America'.[2] The argument, like the general one in Maclean's pamphlet, 'The Coming War With America', formed an important part in his own growing feeling throughout 1920 that Scotland needed a separate Communist Party to ensure that Scotland was not drawn into his anticipated struggle between American and British imperialism.

Developments closer to home, bringing further conflicts with the CPGB, were to intensify that necessity. The rapid development of unemployment in the autumn of 1920 had been predicted by Maclean as an inevitable consequence of trying to squeeze the inflation, associated with excess paper money, out of the system. He had previously preached that 'socialists everywhere . . . ought to organise, lecture and drill the unemployed, and so create a mighty menace to capitalism'.[3] Accordingly Maclean was quick to establish the Glasgow Unemployed Committee with a programme of meetings, lectures and demonstrations designed to pressure the local authority into providing food and shelter. This requirement was particularly acute in Scotland, where special peculiarities in the law and in the disposition of the bureaucracy made it difficult for relief to be provided.

Following the decision of the CLP in October to seek affiliation to the CPGB, J. R. Campbell sought to organise and develop an unemployed agitation in Glasgow which would employ the tactics of direct action to 'seize' work. To that end he tried to take control of the committee from Maclean and his supporters. Having failed in this approach he then established a rival unemployed agitation through the Clyde Workers' Committee. For Maclean this further emphasised the gap between himself and Gallacher: 'The Gallacher gang thrice tried to seize control out of my hands, and failed absolutely.'[4] The conflict provides a demonstration of the failure of the CPGB, as yet, to find a coherent ideological identity. In an oscillation away from its more usual opportunism Campbell's line was an adventuristic posture of direct action and seizure of work. Not for the first time Maclean urged caution and the need 'to exhaust every constitutional method of safeguarding the unemployed'[5]. One of the most misleading caricatures of Maclean is that of an ultra-Left eternally overestimating the revolutionary potential in every situation and urging precipitate and unrealistic action. As with the forty-hours' strike and his later injunction to keep Bellahouston hospital empty, Maclean often showed intensely realistic insight. In this instance he recognised the damage which unemployment had done to working-class morale. His denunciation of *provocateurs* was more than the result of a tactical appreciation, it also fitted Maclean's recurrent strategy, echoed by Lenin, of the need to expose the Labour Party to its working-class audience. Adventurist tactics at this point would have ensured the defeat of the Labour Party at the local elections:

> To rush a work just now would mean split heads and a defeat for the Labour candidates. To use the misfortunes of the unemployed to increase those misfortunes is pitiable, but at the same time to defeat Labour is positively criminal. A Labour Town Council will respond to our pressures more readily than a bourgeois one. If Labour fails then a forceful revolutionary fight is the logical next stage. Unemployment has not really begun yet, neither has the Winter. There is ample time for desperate deeds before the Winter is over if other and more 'constitutional' means fail.[6]

Once again Maclean's mind was turned in the direction of establishing a separate Scottish Communist Party in opposition to that of 'poets and demagogues and deserters of the cause on the outbreak of war'.[7] His first clear commitment to that prospect had been in the September issue of the *Vanguard*, coinciding with the establishment of the CLP; 'Come together, comrades, into the Scottish Communist Council of Action as a first step to a clear and clean S.C [*sic*] Party.' The inseparable issue of an independent Scotland[8] had been hinted at in previous issues in articles on the Irish question and the pamphlet, 'All Hail, the Scottish Workers' Republic', was probably written in August 1920. In November after the débâcle of the second conference of the CLP, he returned to the theme, citing the 'corruption of the London Communists and the position of the English governing class' as justification.[9]

On 25 December 1920 Maclean convened a conference of all those who favoured 'the gist of the "Twenty-One Points"' to 'form a Scottish Communist Party to represent the marxian communism in Scotland'[10]. This meeting, at the SLP rooms in Renfrew Street, finally broke up in disorder.[11] The disaster is usually blamed on the near-brawls between Gallacher on the one side and Maclean and Macdougall on the other. The whole issue of Maclean's not going to Russia and Gallacher's description of his 'hallucinations' was rehearsed and created 'angry scenes'. The substantial grounds for Maclean's failure was the adament refusal of the SLP to support any nationalist initiative. Faced with this resistance he backed away from the idea and appealed to all honest Marxians to rally to the SLP. Maclean followed his own advice during 1921 and, up to his imprisonment, described himself as a 'fighting member' of the SLP. The *Vanguard* was discontinued and Maclean's articles appeared in the *Socialist*, including the 'Open Letter to Lenin' and an important analysis of government strategy called 'Scottish History in the Making'.[12] It is clear that the national question was not of sufficient significance to prevent this co-operation with the implacably anti-nationalist SLP.

The unemployed agitation continued in the spring of 1921. In fact this issue, together with the omnipresent concern with the Scottish Labour College, was Maclean's central campaigning area for the rest of his life. Approximately half of this was to be spent in Barlinnie Prison. The two sentences handed down to

Maclean came in spite of a distinct shift in tone. He had already noted that the defeat of the forty-hours' strike, followed by growing unemployment, had thrown the revolutionary movement into reverse. Whatever message Lenin was receiving about the industrial situation in Britain the reality was quite different:

> Gallacher . . . has led you to believe that there is a workshop movement in Scotland. That is a black lie. I have been at work gates all summer and autumn up and down the Clyde valley, and I am positive when I say that victimisation after the premature forty-hours strike crushed the workshop movement. Unemployment today has struck terror into the hearts of those at work, as starvation is meant to tame the workless. No industrial movement of a radical character is possible at present outside the ranks of the miners, and that movement has been revived and is being carried on by S.L.P.'ers.
>
> I am of the belief that the workshop movement in England is as dead as it is in Scotland.[13]

In this situation Maclean pictured the government as provocative, anxious to incite the revolutionary elements, associate the communists with Sinn Fein and 'to give us a taste of Paris at the end of the Commune'.[14] This analysis had already dictated the tactics of the unemployed movement and Maclean was keen to discourage adventurist moves. He claimed that he was himself exercising an unusual self-restraint, refusing 'to play Lloyd George's game'. Even the *Daily Record* on 14 April had noticed the 'new note' in Maclean's 'public utterances', with his warnings to avoid demonstrations which would allow the authorities to use violent methods of repression: 'This is no plea for passive starvation, but for refusal to resort to childish displays of petty force when the government is ready to give us a deluge of blood. Keep Bellahouston Hospital empty, and you are bringing our victory many days nearer'.[15]

In spite of this, a spate of arrests and seizures followed the killing of an Inspector of Police in Glasgow during an attempt to rescue a Sinn Fein prisoner. The premises of the Scottish Labour College were raided; Tom Mitchell, the SLP secretary and editor of the *Socialist*, was arrested and some days later came the turn of Ross and Maclean. They were tried on 17 May at Airdrie on eleven counts for incitement and sedition. Maclean predictably took the opportunity to make a propaganda speech from the dock, distinguishing between the revolution he advocated and exhortations to violence. In response to an enquiry from the Fiscal as to what he meant by 'revolution', Maclean placed one hand above the other to represent class structure and then reversed the position of the hands. Both defendants received three months. On this occasion Maclean benefited from many of the privileges associated with political prisoners: he was allowed his own clothes and food as well as books and newspapers. The prison authorities noted that 'Maclean is in his usual health but it is not desirable that he should have more cause for excitement than can be avoided'.[16]

He was released on 17 August and resumed his usual activities, which resulted in his re-arrest on 22 September. Remanded in custody to Duke Street prison, he went on hunger strike in protest against the refusal to grant him bail. There was some discussion about recalling Dr Garrey from Peterhead to force-feed Maclean and demands that the trial be brought forward as quickly as possible. The files also express surprise that bail was not granted since the idea that Maclean might abscond before his trial was unthinkable. In the event Maclean's trial was held on 25 October.[17] McShane had previously been tried on the day of Maclean's release and on 18 October MacDougall was given sixty days. The charges at Maclean's trial again included sedition, specifically that he had associated himself with advice given to the unemployed by Ross that if they could not get food legally, they should take it. The trial followed its predictable course but the sentence of twelve months seemed surprisingly harsh to many, particularly since the jury thought it was not his intention to incite to violence. According to the files Maclean did not undertake a hunger strike, much to the obvious relief of the prison authorities: 'Maclean requires a certain amount of humouring in small matters, being daft, in order to make him manageable; . . . he has since his conviction conformed to the Rule for Prisoners . . . and has taken his food'.[18]

During his brief spell 'outside', a shift in electoral tactics had been endorsed. The Labour Party's ineffectual response to the unemployed agitation now justified their being opposed in the November local elections. McShane would stand in Kingston and Maclean in Kinning Park. In the event Maclean's election address had to be issued from Duke Street Prison and he was in Barlinnie when the election itself took place. Despite this, Maclean, describing himself as 'Communist', came a good second to the Moderate and easily beat the Labour candidate into third place.

While in Barlinnie prison, Maclean was effectively again accorded the privileges of a 'political – the humouring in small matters'. His imprisonment also provoked the usual 'large number of resolutions from Labour bodies demanding his release'.[19] In December the Scottish Office received a note from Lloyd George asking for information on the case and about the possibility of remission. But it was felt that the trial had been extensive and the verdict secure enough to rule out any immediate idea of an early release.[20] Perhaps the most interesting feature of this imprisonment are the letters written to his family and James Clunie which have been preserved and then used by MacDiarmid, Nan Milton, Broom and Clunie himself as positive refutation of the rumours circulated by the Communist Party that he was mentally unbalanced. 'Because of the date of the last letter and the period covered by the series, the first being dated 25/11/1921, there is clear evidence that the impression set abroad by people, many of whom were indebted to him, that John Maclean was latterly mentally ill was completely untrue.'[21]

It is certainly true that the letters to Clunie,[22] and even more to his family, convey every impression of good humour, balance and a sense of perspective. The demands placed on Clunie for reading material show that typically voracious appetite for knowledge on a wide variety of subjects – physics and biology alongside economics and current affairs. It is, however, also possible to discern a shift in style and tone in the letters written while in Barlinnie and those written in 1923, several months after his release from prison. These were Maclean's last months, a period of growing personal hardship and overwork. We would suggest in an amateur and tentative observation that the sureness of touch and realism which characterised Maclean were beginning to fail. The perspective of the world outside Glasgow seems to fade and is replaced by an obsessiveness about his own progress and that of his party for which claims are made which future events hardly confirm. It is, of course, partly a reflection of the amount of working hours he was devoting to the task. To the very end there was a crescendo of relentless activity.

Following his release from prison, Maclean embarked on an electoral campaign in Kinning Park for the local election and was a candidate for the Gorbals constituency in the general election, also held in November 1922. This time his scanty organisational resources were even thinner on the ground. McShane had accepted what he saw as the inevitable and had joined the CPGB;[23] Ross had departed for India and MacDougall had suffered a nervous collapse following his spell in prison. Of the Tramps Trust, only Peter Marshall remained in loyal support. It also appears that Maclean's association with the SLP was not resumed after his imprisonment. This was probably inevitable, as the latter organisation had clearly been badly damaged by the secessions first of the Communist Unity Group, then of the Communist Labour Party. Its reaction appears to have been to sink back into a dogmatic, de Leonist sectarianism from which it had once emerged under the pressure of the war and the October Revolution.

In spite of his isolation Maclean demonstrated the relevance of his personal following, at least in Glasgow. The local elections in Kinning Park again saw Maclean coming a good second with 4,287 votes, whilst in the Gorbals Parliamentary election he polled 4,027, well behind George Buchanan's 16,479 for the Labour Party, but 'hardly the vote of an irrelevant romantic sectarian'.[24] A full-blooded, revolutionary election address to the 'Wage Slave Class' from a 'Bolshevik, alias a Communist, alias a Revolutionist, alias a Marxian'[25] was not aimed at maximising short-term support. The vituperative personal abuse (particularly of Gallacher), the determination to discuss the crisis of international capitalism rather than domestic issues, and the declaration of intent to boycott Westminster were ill-suited to the faint-hearted or uncommitted. Indeed Maclean's advice to them was to vote for Buchanan if they felt unable to stomach the full programme.

Certainly electoral support for the Labour Party had grown since 1918. The results in 1922 throughout industrial Scotland reflected the increasing dominance of Labour in the form of the ILP on Clydeside. Against this Maclean had started in the Gorbals 'without committee, money or anything'.[26] On all the crucial issues, housing, unemployment, pensions, the Labour Party, with its superior resources and its apparent relevance, was the dominant force. Even Maclean's stance on Ireland or Scottish independence had been pre-empted by a paler and vaguer version. The ebbing of the tide of revolution and militancy was likely, in itself, to enhance the electoral prospects and relevance of the Labour Party.

The battle which Maclean believed could yet be won was the one for dominance of the revolutionary Left at least in Glasgow and perhaps in Scotland. The ground on which it was fought included his beloved Scottish Labour College. Repeated efforts to establish and re-establish the College had been complicated by ambitions to make the institution more 'respectable' academically. Such ideas usually involved fusion with the Plebs League, various degrees of association with the WEA or even extra-mural arrangements with universities.[27] Any such initiatives found Maclean as the major obstacle. He was concerned to maintain an independence which would guarantee its unequivocally agitational character, modelled on his own celebrated pre-war and post-war economics classes. An interesting sidelight to this conflict, in view of the subsequent debate on the character of Maclean's nationalism, was the flank attack by Erskine and an Aberdeen trade unionist, Diack, on the absence of Scottish history with a definite national identity.

While Maclean was in prison the CPGB had intensified its efforts to remove him and gain control of the College. These efforts had been a major factor in the spleen directed against Gallacher in his 1922 election address. At the start of 1923 the spearhead of the offensive was J. C. P. Millar, a Communist Party member from Edinburgh. In January the National Committee asked Maclean to draft a constitution, but actually accepted the rival one from Millar. Maclean promptly severed his connection with the institution, adding yet another sense of treachery and betrayal to his already overflowing cup of bitterness. The exclusion of any possibility of an income from this source may have prompted him to renew his application for reinstatement as a teacher at this time. It was also an attempt to reassure his still estranged wife, Agnes, that he could provide a normal enough home for the upbringing of his two daughters. But even here, Maclean found it necessary to belabour the School Board with an account of the events surrounding his earlier dismissal which, he argued, proved him to have been in the right.[28]

In the meantime, as one long-cherished project crumbled to

dust, he launched another. On 23 February he finally announced the foundation of his Scottish Workers' Republican Party. According to the SLP's historian the bulk of the recruits were defectors from that organisation.[29] Harry McShane was later to refer to 'queer people that I didn't like' who 'knew nothing about socialism or revolutionary work'.[30] Even retrospectively this is not an impartial source; nor is the contemporary opinion of the ILP whom David Howell quotes from *Forward*:

> if mere talking could bring us nearer the Scottish Commonwealth, then the Socialist Workers' Republican Party are the fellows to get us there at record speed. If facility in the use of 'dams' [sic] and 'bloodies' and other choice epithets could do it, they would have us there already. But the S.W.R.P. have been at the job for some time now, and as their practical achievements on behalf of the workers are so far nil, it would appear that windy oratory and bad language are not the chosen instruments of the social revolution.[31]

That the above picture is not wholly misleading, however, is suggested by the single set of surviving branch minutes in the National Library of Scotland, and Howell again demonstrates one instance where even Maclean was not totally 'happy with his recruits'.[32]

This party occupied the last months of Maclean's life, and the parochial scale of its operations were in sharp contrast to the heady days of the past and to some of Maclean's rhetoric in 1923. The first in a series of local elections fought during the year was his own candidature in the thirtieth ward. Describing himself as 'COMMUNIST or RED LABOUR' he introduced the notion of extending the city into a provincial council controlling the whole Clyde Valley 'so as to enable the workers more adequately to control all the industries in this very clearly defined area'.[33] The limits on the powers and scope of the corporation imposed by the Westminster Parliament were suggested as a further reason for advocating Scottish independence. It was not enough to convince a majority of the electors.

In the meantime, of course, the unemployed agitation went on and gave rise to the affair of the Helen Street Cinema in Govan. The manager, James Hamilton, had been permitting meetings on this issue to be held on Sunday evenings in the cinema. He was eventually dismissed for this practice and was replaced by Tom Collins, a local Labour councillor. Maclean and his associates organised a boycott of the cinema, parading and holding nightly demonstrations outside. In the end Hamilton was reinstated but Maclean and another SWRP member, Thomas Macgregor, were arrested for using words likely to provoke a breach of the peace. The trial resulted in a guilty verdict and a fine which Maclean predictably refused to pay.[34] It seems that when the police attempted to arrest him Maclean informed the constable that he had arranged to leave for Ireland that very day and was allowed to do so.[35] No further action appears to have been forthcoming.

During the same period as the Helen Street boycott, Maclean seems to have been involved with the Unity Committee described by Tom Anderson as 'composed of, all the "left wing organisations" of the City'.[36] From a perusal of the delegates it seems to have been an SWRP/SLP front with the ostensible aim of organising an industrial union body for the whole of Glasgow. Maclean produced a document for its May Day Appeal under the title 'Workers Now for Industrial Unity', but little else seems to have emerged from the 'front'. The line is, of course, highly reminiscent of one of the SLP's central concerns. Though Maclean himself never placed the same priority on industrial unionism he was always deeply aware of the inherent sectional appeal of traditional trade union disputes. Whether it was minimum wages or maximum hours or campaigns on rents and prices there was always the anxiety to devise slogans and activity which could generalise an agitation across the internal boundaries of the working class.

The SWRP was now fighting in every local by-election and in June Maclean stood in the Kingston Ward. In North Kelvin, O'Donnell, an existing candidate, joined the Party and ran in the name of the SWRP. They were faced by opposition from the Trades Council, the Labour Party, the ILP, and the CPGB, who were also supporting the Labour candidate in the name of its united front tactics. Maclean also noted grimly the presence, among his opponents, of Harry McShane. The Moderate, Armstrong, won in Kingston with 3,169 votes but Maclean beat Labour's Peter Campbell into third place by 2,008 votes to 1,865. The tone of Maclean's subsequent comments suggest that he regarded the latter as the main battle.[37] One product of his regular visits to Ireland during this period was Countess Markiewicz speaking three times in his support during the campaign.

Despite Maclean's bitterness at McShane's 'betrayal', his response when the latter was evicted from his home in Gorbals was one of instant solidarity. The SWRP held a march to his house and also made a collection for Thomas Hitman, also of the CPGB, who was in prison awaiting trial. The following Sunday saw a further procession outside Duke Street Prison where the crowd shouted 'Free Tom Hitman'. Whether as a result of this or otherwise, it appears that Hitman changed his party affiliation and was standing as an SWRP candidate for Calton in the November municipal elections. Before that, in July, Maclean contested Townhead, his 'first burst into the north side of the river'.[38] As he conceded, the SWRP committee was 'young and inexperienced' and Maclean came third. The tone of a letter to Clunie after the election again reveals an intense hostility to the Labour Party and great satisfaction in the fact that MacGregor's vote had plunged to fifty per cent of the previous Labour vote in November. The argument, such as it is, in his correspondence with Clunie at this period is that capitalism is out of control and is plunging to disaster: reactionaries are sweeping to power politicalically but the next swing will be to the extreme left creating a 'situation calling us into power'.

It is clear that towards the end of his life Maclean's domestic situation was catastrophic. Agnes was still unwilling to return, angry that her husband refused to consider a tutorship at the Labour College. Maclean was entirely unwilling to accept the condition, imposed by the Glasgow district, that the tutor should withdraw from active political agitation. He had no income and both food and clothing were inadequate. When Baillie George Smith accused him, on the grounds of the SWRP's attacks on the Labour Party, of being in the pay of the Moderates, Maclean suggested grimly to his wife, 'I think you might write him and tell him how much I get!' Despite these difficulties Maclean's rate of activity never slackened and it is clear that the strain was beginning to show. His extreme assertions seemed to take the character of incantation, were unsupported by analysis and unleavened by shafts of humour. At the last his acuteness of observation seemed to be deserting him. There are no major articles of Marxist analysis surviving from this latter period. From the end of the summer Maclean's efforts were directed to the local elections in November.

The SWRP proposed a slate of twelve candidates, all their public speakers, as he admitted to Clunie.[39] The CPGB, in the name of its united front tactics, attacked them through the medium of the *Worker*.

> We understand that Labour candidates in various districts are going to be opposed by S.W.R.P. candidates, a pack of political ragamuffins whose only qualification appears to be a brass face, and a complete ignorance of working class political tactics. This deplorable exhibition of vanity is taking place at a time when the baby-starvers are contemplating the reduction of the parish dole. Every vote they

take away from the Labour candidate is strengthening the Moderates. Every Labour defeat they cause will hearten the baby-starver.[40]

It is a familiar argument, familiar at least to Maclean who had used a variant of it against Campbell and the *Worker* during the battles for control of the unemployed agitation in 1920. It is just possible to argue, as he did, that the Clydesiders of 1922 had exposed their impotence and ineffectiveness at Westminster in the brief period since the election. Most of the time Maclean scarcely bothers. His growing hostility to the 'Pinks' merely becomes more strident as his circumstances deteriorate. He had, in 1922, advised the electors who could not bring themselves to vote for him to vote for George Buchanan. There is no repetition of such advice either in the municipal elections in November nor in his later campaign in the Gorbals in the general election. The campaign for Labour was reinforced by the arrival of Smillie and George Lansbury, eminent figures who Maclean had known and respected in the past.

Their presence may have been sufficient provocation to create a *de facto* alliance between Maclean and Sylvia Pankhurst, lately expelled from the CPGB for refusing to subordinate the *Workers' Dreadnought* to party discipline. Her latest enthusiasm was to attack the Poplar Guardians of the Poor whose chairman was Edgar Lansbury, George's nephew. Already beleaguered by the district auditors, the Poplar Guardians had called the police to evict an unemployed demonstration from the Council Chambers earning themselves the unyielding hostility of the super intransigent, Pankhurst. The SWRP issued a leaflet attacking the Guardians and the Poplar ILP derisively, claiming that 'Three years late they are all laying emphasis on unemployment to catch votes.'[41] The following week Sylvia Pankhurst arrived in Glasgow to support the campaign of Maclean and the SWRP. She returned from Glasgow seriously worried about Maclean's health and life-style:

'he lived quite alone, doing his own cooking and housework; a greater hardship this for the strenuous agitator ... speaking continuously in all weathers ... He was talking enthusiastically of the nourishing properties of pease flour poridge when last we saw him.'[42]

In fact Maclean's wife did finally return to him on 17 November in time to plead unavailingly with him to withdraw his candidature for the Gorbals in the general election. Predictably, Maclean continued with his campaign, despite not having enough money to pay the deposit. The election issue was, of course, Baldwin's appeal for a mandate to levy tariffs on a range of imported goods. Maclean stood on neither side of this issue:

> Neither Free Trade nor Protection is of use to the Workers. Taxation of land or capital, including the Capital Levy, is of no use to the workers. No housing or other social reform is really possible while industry is paralysed and the earnings of the workers are ever shrinking. The only possible hope of the working class is Community Ownership of the means of production. The increasing poverty and misery in Gorbals ought to convince the most conservative workers that all the 'Woolworth' pottering of the petty politicians of all the 'practical' parties (the Labour Party included) has brought no improvement into the life of the citizens of the Gorbals.[43]

For Scotland it would be the 'wisest policy' to declare for a Republic, both to prevent the use of Scottish youth in British colonial wars and to extort concessions from the Westminster Parliament. It might be noticed that this is to use the threat of independence to achieve something else.

> So you sent George Buchanan to get your rents back. Buchanan and his friends have spent a fruitless year and have returned home empty of hand. So, after all, I was right. Had the Labour men stayed in Glasgow and started a Scottish Parliament, as did the genuine Irish in Dublin in 1918, England would have sat up and made

concessions to Scotland, just to keep her ramshackle Empire intact to bluff other countries.[44]

The whole question of nationalism is one we propose to return to but the argument illustrates yet again Maclean's determination, throughout 1923, to expose and attack the Labour Party, heedless of the short-term consequences. His hostility to, and scorn for, the people he alternatively called 'Pinks' or 'Woolworth politicians', in an allusion to their cheap opportunism and vote-scrounging, has clear echoes throughout the contemporary history of the Labour Party. The final election leaflet, penned by Maclean, which also warned: 'Beware the Fascisti . . . in country after country',[45] caricatured a Labour Party with which we are familiar: 'Just now Baldwin was reforming capitalism, trapping the Pinks who played on mothers' milk, housing rents and other reform superficialities to gain popular support so as to make Ramsay Macdonald or Clynes, Prime Minister of Britain'.[46]

Maclean did not reach election day. Years of frenetic activity interspersed with imprisonment finally exacted their price. A throat infection, months old, was exacerbated by speaking, coatless, out of doors in the November rain and fog. On 25 November he had to abandon a meeting at the Rex Cinema, Rutherglen Road because of a coughing attack. He soon developed a chill which deteriorated into pneumonia and, on the morning of 30 November, he died aged forty-four. The funeral was held on 3 December and Maclean's own personal standing was reflected in the attendance of some 10,000 people. He left behind a disputed heritage, the divisions only temporarily obscured by the conventional stampede to express laudatory obituaries across the left-wing press. Guy Aldred declared himself 'wearied and dissatisfied at the tributes paid in death that, were the dead to rise, would be withdrawn and replaced by gibes . . . Even Gallacher has forgotten what he said in detriment of the dead warrior a few weeks before his passing.'[47]

7 A Scottish patriot?

The picture of Maclean has been obscured and distorted over the years rather than being brought into clearer focus. In particular the claims relating to Maclean's commitment to a separate Communist Party for Scotland have created a misleading legend. The Scottish Workers' Republican Party was the creation of Maclean's alleged espousal of the cause of Scottish nationalism. We have already seen the unequivocally hostile reception it was awarded by its contemporary rivals on the Left. This was only to be expected. By and large it has had a similarly bad press from retrospective memoirs and academic histories alike – even where the assessment of Maclean is sympathetic. 'Apart from him, the Party had no significance', says David Howell.[1] I. S. McLean is unequivocal: 'The "Scottish Workers' Republican Party" which he founded was not a success; it fought no elections and did not long outlive him'.[2] An ex-member, John Mitchell, says that the Party 'got off to a bad start and folded up a few months after the premature death of Maclean at forty-four years of age'.[3] Even if these statements could be accepted at face value the SWRP would have fared no worse than any of the other revolutionary organisations who did not have the CPGB'S access to financial blood transfusions.

In fact the SWRP fought several elections, both before and after Maclean's death. Apart from his own parliamentary campaign in the Gorbals in 1923 and the four local elections already described, other members fought one local election in June and eleven in November. The party was still fighting in at least four wards in 1931[4] and had certainly fought one in 1928.[5] There may well have been more. Apart from their electoral activity, the 'claymore communists', as the CPGB dubbed them, were involved in the free-speech agitation on Glasgow Green in 1924.[6] An SWRP manifesto was issued in the following year and in 1927 the party began the publication of a monthly paper. At least forty-six issues of the *Scottish Workers' Republic* were produced up to August 1932 and perhaps later, since that month's issue was boasting of increased membership and announcing its plans for the re-publication of Maclean's writings in pamphlet form. The repeated invocation of the name of 'the founder', observance of anniversaries and so on, is not the only claim to continuity. Prominent activists such as Edward Rennie, Peter McIntyre and John Ball were founder members along with Maclean and continued to reflect some of the characteristic lines.

There may be an inherent paradox in Maclean's own determination to maintain unswerving loyalty to the Soviet State, the October Revolution and the Comintern whilst attacking implacably the latter's own offspring in Great Britain. It emerges in an unconscious form when the SWRP, itself a kind of 'left opposition' in domestic terms, is obliged to comment on the exile of Trotsky:

> We are sorry that such drastic steps should have been necessary but we can well see, there was no other course open to the Workers' Government, than to protect the revolution. Great men think themselves greater than the 'mass' and thus they are unable to fall into line when the 'mass' dictates the policy. Once relinquish the 'Dictatorship of the Proletariat' and the bourgeois [*sic*] would step in: possibly Trotsky will be used by the 'Whites' for this purpose, he will not have been the first.
>
> The maintenance of the Revolution, is of more importance than all the great men on the earth. The day will come when all these men will be dead.[7]

Did anyone in the CPGB mutter a similar formula when Maclean was 'slipped out' in 1920? The SWRP were careful to follow in all matters the gospel according to 'the founder' in so far as they understood it. On occasion, this can appear as an inflexible caricature of Maclean's position. The abstentionist tactic adopted by him in 1922-23 is elevated into something close to an anti-Parliamentarist principle. The constitution of the SWRP published in 1927 contains no structure or organisation and their absence is justified in extraordinary fashion: 'In consequence, subservient worship of rigid rules and regulations of Party but helps the enemy in the same way as participation in capitalist legislatures such as Parliament etc.'[8]

Of the greatest concern to the debate on Maclean's inheritance is the reflected light which the SWRP sheds on Maclean's original line on the national independence issue. On the one hand, both the 1925 manifesto and the party constitution propound a somewhat defensive statement of a nationalist posture, arguing that it is 'no more inconsistent with Internationalism than is the demand for a Workers' Republic for India, Egypt or Ireland'.[9] On the other hand, the dozen or so monthly issues of the paper, which we have been able to read, contain no references to the national question apart from a single disparaging article on the inadequacies of 'home rulers'. The central themes are attacks on the 'Parliamentary road', gradualism and the united front: 'Our advice to the C.P. is get off your knees and stop crawling to the Labour Party and concentrate upon getting your organisation into a clean and healthy revolutionary position.'[10]

A recurrent argument is that trade disputes or other 'fights against the effects of capitalism' are not to be mistaken for gains in themselves but are to be regarded as the gaining of experience for the overthrow of capitalism itself. One item in particular is extremely revealing of how the Scottish independence issue is scarcely relevant for the SWRP. In 1928, a long editorial posed the question, 'The General Election – Shall We Vote?' The anti-Parliamentarians, it observed, would be advising the boycott of the ballot whilst the CPGB would recommend voting Communist in one place and Labour in another. Maclean's principle was then explained:

> the founder of the SWRP, Comrade John Maclean M.A., gave the answer to that question in his 1922 Parliamentary Address to the Gorbals. He said, 'If you cannot vote for me then vote for the Labour Candidate.'

> As well as opposing the Labour politicians because they could not do other than mislead the people for the sake of £400 a year, he had no objection to allowing them to prove his words with a majority in Parliament . . . But someone might say, 'this is just what the C.P. of G.B. think. Maclean therefore had no right to organise another Party.'[11]

One might expect, at this point, that advocates of Scottish independence would produce the obvious national reason for organising a specifically Scottish Communist Party, but not one word emerges to this effect. Instead, there follows a denunciatory review of Communist Party history from *Left Wing Communism* onwards, itemising its crawling for affiliation to the Labour Party, its support for Henderson, the murderer of James Connolly, etc., etc. These, it claimed, were the antics which had disgusted Maclean. The argument is not very subtle and neither is the version of Maclean's differences with the CPGB, but it does reflect, accurately enough, the place of the independence issue in the priorities of the SWRP and its founder. The whole balance of the paper presents a sharp contrast to that of the *Scots Socialist* of the 1930s and 1940s where the proportion of Marxism to nationalism is inverse. This paper, like the much later *Scottish Vanguard,* has attempted to claim Maclean for their own nationalist perspective, an outlook which, the evidence suggests, neither he nor his immediate followers ever shared.

James Clunie, one of the closest associates of John Maclean's later years, has stated: 'His party, The Scottish Workers' Republican Party, was created out of extremity, more an instrument with which he could attack his enemy than as a movement to bear fruit'.[12] With some modification, we believe that such a notion can be usefully applied to Maclean's whole involvement with Scottish nationalism. This particular aspect of Maclean's later career has loomed large because, unlike the slur that he was mentally unbalanced, it can be shared by friends and detractors alike. On the one hand, some orthodox Marxists have found it a simple explanation for his apparently aberrant refusal to join the CPGB while on the other, a kind of Scottish New Left has been able to appropriate him to its own brand of neo-nationalism. This latter process has been aided and abetted by Nan Milton[13] and swallowed whole by James Hinton.[14]

David Howell, in the most valuable assessment yet, is inclined to go some way down this road. 'Maclean had an awareness of his identity that was specifically Scottish.' He 'claimed the existence of a Celtic identity when expressing his hopes that Scotland could emulate and ally with Ireland . . . Moreover, Maclean had a relatively uncritical perception of Scottish identity – and held to an uncomplicated belief in distinctive racial characteristics.'[15] In these attitudes Maclean is compared with Connolly, though a difference in degree is acknowledged. We believe that it is significant that Maclean *never* cites Connolly or his arguments, with which he was wholly familiar, in support of his position. The particular language of *'All Hail The Scottish Workers' Republic'* should be seen in the context of the host of Maclean's other writings, which are dissimilar in style. It was written under the pressure of an extreme crisis in the affairs of Ireland and Sinn Fein. In any case, Socialists of the period were not at all inhibited – witness Marx and Engels everywhere – by fashionable obsessions about anti-racism from making intelligent racial generalisations. Most often, as in a letter to his daughters at Christmas 1922, Maclean put these into a clear class context: 'Your business as Socialists is to remember that all the people of the world are as good as any other . . . The English are worse and wickeder than the French are supposed to be because the wealthy class are greedier.'[16]

A wholly different posture has been adopted by, for example, I. S. McLean, who argues that Maclean's alleged nationalism is hardly worthy of discussion because it was 'pragmatic', not orthodox, and always subordinate to his Marxism.[17] We believe that the accuracy of these epithets make the position all the more intriguing. His stance on independence was reiterated too often and too clearly to be other than a serious and considered one. He did take a nationalist position that cannot be dismissed because it is subordinate to a greater principle. Lenin's advice on national questions in general is well known, as is his view that Irish nationalism was to be supported. The question – about which Lenin knew nothing – of whether Scotland was an exploited nation and, above all, whether a genuine, mass, nationalist sentiment existed, was not a simple judgement. Neither conclusion is absurd, from a Marxist point of view as long as, like Maclean's it is contingent on concrete circumstances.

We have already argued that the national issue was not the cause of his estrangement from the BSP/CPGB and that it was not of primary political importance either to Maclean or to the SWRP. His quarrel with the embryo Communist Party was already well under way before he espoused the notion for the first time.[18] Previously he had been entirely content to conduct his politics in an all-British context. Nan Milton herself quotes an earlier expression of Maclean's, in *Justice* (27 July 1912), 'those curious cranks whimsically styled "The Scottish Patriots"', though, of course, she claims that the disdain was reserved for a moderate brand of 'home rulers'.[19]

In reality Maclean's growing hostility towards the Communist Party being launched in Great Britain presented him with a considerable dilemma. Though opposed to these developments he remained wholly loyal to the Bolshevik Revolution, its leaders and the Comintern. This included the principle, laid down in the seventeenth point of the Theses and Statutes of the Third International, that there should be only one Communist Party in each country. Since Maclean wanted a different one to the CPGB, the discovery that Scotland was a separate country was the way of squaring the circle. This point is made explicitly on more than one occasion.

The solution was the more attractive because of several other circumstances pushing in the same direction. Probably the most important of these were events in Ireland. The Rebellion of 1916, the execution of James Connolly, and the Black and Tans were traumatic for all British revolutionaries but especially for those in Glasgow. Connolly's personal connections with the city and with Maclean, as well as the high level of activity by the numerous Sinn Fein branches, cried loudly for an act of solidarity. The balance of attention in Maclean's public writings at the time showed how deeply the Irish situation affected him, and in November 1922 he wrote to President Cosgrove to protest against the executions of four Republicans by the new Free State Government and the possibility that others might follow, including Erskine Childers.[20] Moreover, Maclean was convinced that a war between Britain and America, the world's leading imperialist powers, was imminent. Since the Scottish coast was crucial to British contingency plans, the principle of revolutionary defeatism, applied in advance, would encompass a nationalist strategy. Indeed the possibility of such a war was given by Maclean as the principal reason for urging the creation of a Scottish Workers' Republic. In an article 'The Clyde and the general election' published by the *Socialist* in December 1922 Maclean wrote:

> Where a Red like myself stood against a Pink . . . I refused to talk on rent taxes, levies and such minor issues. I centred on the French and American obstruction to British trade revival, the hopeless breakdown of John Bull's trade and empire, and the risk of another world war, unless the world went through the Revolution . . . as the first step to World Communism . . . To avert war, or to keep Scotland out of it, I urged a Scottish Workers' Republic . . . in furtherance of that goal my plan was to stay in their midst . . . refusing to go to London.[21]

The Irish example inspired Maclean with the notion of striking a blow at the very heart of British imperialism, which he always claimed was the world's greatest obstacle to the communist revolution and the major threat to Soviet Russia. He challenged Scottish socialist critics of the Sinn Feiners with the assertion that Sinn Fein, without any socialist motivation, had done more to break up the British Empire than all the socialists in Britain. But he was not blind to the political deficiencies of the Sinn Feiners and warned them that unless their struggle was located in a wider international socialist context it would be to no avail. Maud Gonne MacBride, wife of the executed leader Sean Mac-Bride and object of Yeats's devotion, heard Maclean on this theme and wrote to inform him that it had entirely changed her view of the Irish struggle for national independence.[22] At the same time Maclean was also convinced that the cause of international social revolution was further advanced in Scotland than in England. These considerations were all real and attested by his public utterances. They did not make nationalism the central feature of his philosophy. The tendency to allocate it such a role has served to divert attention from the depth of his disagreement with the strategies of the CPGB. A small illustration of this is offered in the pamphlet, 'John Maclean and Scottish Independence,' where Nan Milton writes that the less advanced revolutionary feeling in England 'was naturally reflected in the outlook of the majority of the E.C. (of the B.S.P.) members who were, of course, English. Policies which suited English conditions rather than Scottish ones were adopted in a perfectly democratic manner.'[23]

The argument is one which Maclean never used. It is certain that he did not regard the policies to which he was opposed as suited to England any better than to Scotland; he repeatedly made clear that the manner by which they were adopted was deeply suspect rather than 'perfectly democratic'.

Even after twice trying and failing to establish a Scottish Communist Party, Maclean felt able to join the SLP, a party which ridiculed and rejected the notion of 'a Communist Party for pure Scotsmen'. Neither Maclean nor the SLP abandoned their respective positions and the former occasionally argued his case in the columns of the *Socialist*. The issue was simply not of sufficient importance to inhibit their cohabitation for nearly two years, from January 1921 to October 1922. At this later date, on his release from prison, Maclean parted from the SLP which, he claimed, had neither 'fire nor fighters'. His relations with it remained, nevertheless, quite amicable, even surviving the birth of the SWRP, which may have taken several defectors from the SLP. James Clunie, who remained a member, was a close associate and correspondent for the rest of Maclean's life, and several of the letters from Maclean to Clunie indicate the attitude we have described.

In these letters there is a remarkable absence of reference to any national perspectives during 1923.[24] The major political conflict is described throughout as that between the 'Reds' and the 'Pink' and his quarrel with the CPGB continues to be both that it is unprincipled, and that it is 'playing it very dirty'. Typical extracts are:

The C.P. have thus smashed the unemployed movement all over Glasgow and are in consequence of the U.F. with the 'Pinks', smashing their now discredited party.[25]

It's a scream by the way, for the C.P.G.B. here doing dirty work against us in the name of the 'United Front', when the C.P. is compelled to start a rival union in Fife.[26]

All the stewards were C.P. men (at a Trades Council demonstration). So there you have it, the C.P. acting as scavengers for the 'Pinks'. We have ours on Friday and yesterday I had a wire from Sylvia Pankhurst that she's coming on Friday . . . The nominations of our twelve candidates are in and the 'Glasgow Herald' gave a good boost to the 'Red Menace'[27]

Maclean was never 'committed to a romantic Celtic Communism', and James D. Young is right in saying that only one article, of the legion which he wrote, can be so interpreted.[28] Erskine of Marr, the most noted Nationalist, rated more space in the *Socialist*, that inveterate foe of Scots nationalism, than he did in the *Vanguard*. The last word in getting Maclean totally wrong can be left to Hugh McDiarmid, because it is not a very new, new Left, struggling to harness Maclean to neo-nationalism: 'Maclean was on sound and profound Leninist lines and was quite untainted by the Trotskyist exaltation of world revolution instead of getting on with the work immediately to hand'.[29]

The distinction is not one Maclean would even have understood. Each and every justification for his position on Scottish independence was explained in the context of its contribution to that very world revolution. He was, as he always insisted, first, last and always an Internationalist and cannot be properly understood except in that context.

Conclusion

By any conventional standard Maclean's life would be judged a tragic failure. This seems self-evident in that the objects of Maclean's political activities were, and indeed remain unrealised. The revolution to which he devoted himself did not occur, and at the time of his death he lacked even the money to participate as a candidate at the general election of 1923. Moreover he left behind him no lasting political organisation except the SWRP, which remained in being until the 1930s, proclaiming a revolutionary message which owed more to Marxism than nationalism. It served, however, to create an impression of Maclean as being primarily a Scottish phenomenon.

In personal terms Maclean's unceasing commitment to the revolutionary cause over twenty years contributed to the loss of his career as a teacher and certainly left him emotionally exhausted; by 1923 Maclean was a 'burnt-out case'. In addition, Maclean's family life was undermined by his refusal to abandon active political life and he was estranged from his wife from 1919 until near his death, when a reconciliation seemed possible. Certainly Maclean's wife, Agnes, found the strain of his life hard to bear and this contributed to her own indifferent health. At the end of his life, at the early age of forty-four, Maclean was unable to support himself, let alone his wife and two young daughters and this clearly depressed him.

The extent of this failure was sufficiently great to obscure the underlying significance of Maclean as an outstanding, perhaps *the* outstanding British Marxist. It has also contributed to the general confusion over what legacy Maclean has left for the British Left. He was the most important British Social Democrat of the pre-war period to declare his support for the Bolshevik revolution and the Third International. In addition he was the one British Marxist who responded in a clear and independent manner to the breakdown of social democracy in a way which placed him alongside Liebknecht, Luxemburg, Trotsky and even Lenin in seeking a fresh socialist route forward and a new Revolutionary International. His support for the Third International was maintained to the end, notwithstanding his criticisms of the CPGB. He was, then, at all times an Internationalist and cannot be understood outside this context.

Terry Brotherstone, in a recent, timely and thought-provoking piece, emphasises the degree to which Maclean's reputation has been 'consistently, even systematically underestimated or misrepresented'.[1] We would vary this judgement to the effect that Maclean has been misrepresented *and* consequently underestimated. In the main such misrepresentation or at least misunderstanding has focused on the related questions of Maclean's hostility to the CPGB and support for an independent Scotland. In particular the preoccupation with Maclean's 'Scottishness' has distorted much of the recent evaluation of his politics. Indeed it has been the predominant perspective through which Maclean's political life has been viewed.

As we have observed many, if not most, critics and supporters of Maclean have accepted the idea that his commitment to a notion of an independent Scotland was ultimately the distinctive characteristic of his politics. It is a characterisation that we believe to be wrong in its emphasis and damaging in its effects on most assessments of Maclean's political role. The tendency to take the representation of Maclean as a Scottish Nationalist at superficial value, without any close examination of its nature and place in Maclean's political scheme has led too easily and erroneously to the view that his hostility to the CPGB derived from his narrow Scottishness and obsessional suspicion of the London Gang.

It was not a geographical or a national difference which Maclean had with the CPGB but a more fundamental ideological difference over the capacity of that Party and its leaders to pursue an appropriate revolutionary course. It was because he doubted whether the recruits to leading positions had any real understanding of Marxism that he ridiculed what he saw as its preposterous attempt to offer revolutionary leadership to the working class. After all is said, it was a Scot, Willie Gallacher, who came in for some of Maclean's strongest invective for posing as a Marxist when he had always been an Anarcho-syndicalist.

It is the case that more interesting ideas have emerged recently, such as the notion put forward by Bain who has tried to present Maclean's estrangement from the CPGB as anticipating the argument between Stalin and Trotsky, and this is a proposition we find interesting, particularly since we have tentatively suggested a similar kind of relationship in the argument between Maclean and Rothstein over 'Hands off Russia' and the question of 'Socialism in One Country'[2] Such ideas may be provocative and may be disputed, but they promise to take discussion of Maclean beyond the kind of gross misrepresentation found in R. K. Middlemas's *The Clydesiders*, where he says of Maclean, 'He represented . . . the deep rooted tendency towards anarchism which ran through the politics of the extreme left in the early twentieth century and which was still represented in Glasgow between the wars by Guy Aldred.'[3]

In terms of how posterity would treat him, Maclean could scarcely have died at a less auspicious moment. The Bolshevik Revolution was still in its most heroic phase and Maclean had no wish to disassociate himself from it in any way. The Comintern still offered the prospect of developing as a 'genuine', independent International and was again a body with which he was anxious to associate himself. His alienation from the revolutionary communist movement did not extend beyond his sharp critique of the CPGB. Yet that body, on the one side, and the Labour Party, on the other, had appropriated the available political space on the Left. Moreover neither of them had an interest in associating themselves too closely with Maclean, save in the case of the Communists to appropriate his memory as revolutionary martyr.

The fact that Maclean died prior to the historic Stalin–Trotsky struggle meant that he remained something of a problem for British Trotskyists even supposing that they were aware of his existence. For orthodox Trotskyists the failure of Maclean to join the CPGB was a serious error, notwithstanding the validity of his reasons for opposing that Party. His subsequent support for an independent Scotland, though in principle less troublesome for Trotskyists, would have made Maclean a somewhat awkward model when taken together with his absence from the CPGB. Thus someone like Brotherstone, who recognised the importance of Maclean earlier than many socialist historians and has consistently shown sensitivity in approaching his legacy, has nonetheless criticised Maclean for his refusal to join the CPGB.

Taken as a whole Maclean remained a neglected figure amongst revolutionary Socialists until quite recently, when they have reacted to his apparent discovery by the Scottish New Left in ways which have obscured rather than clarified his position as revolutionary Marxist. One of the more prevalent misunderstanding about Maclean is that he was in some sense an ultra-left revolutionary purist whose rigid political outlook was a reflection of his dour personality. This is simply false. Maclean was adamant that Marxism was a living ideology which could be used flexibly to deal with changing material circumstances.

The criticisms laid against Gallacher and Pankhurst by Lenin on this score would have been wholly inappropriate if levelled against Maclean. 'Left-Wing Communism' was a pamphlet that

Maclean would have supported without qualification. Through-out his political career he demonstrated that mixture of revolutionary intransigence and tactical flexibility which we associate most readily with Bolshevism as, for example, when he recognised earlier than most that the possibility for revolutionary action had passed in 1919/20 or when he cautioned that demands for reforms should take precedence over revolutionary sloganis-ing. In fact some of Maclean's strongest criticism of the CPGB was directed at what he saw as its ultra-leftism, especially in campaigns involving the unemployed.

What he always avoided until the last few months of his life was the politics of illusion. He never had any illusions about the backwardness of the working classes and never pandered to it in the manner of the Labour 'Woolworth' politicians whom he despised. Indeed it was in recognition of that backwardness that he never 'watered the wine of his political message' in the words of MacDougall. In practice, then, one of the most striking features of Maclean's politics was his capacity for balancing reformist and revolutionary demands, a complex task which many of his con-temporaries on the revolutionary Left found impossible to man-age. But while Maclean was perceptive in his political analysis of events he was clearly a difficult colleague to work with on occasions. This is not to say that he was unable to maintain political and personal relationships; many such relationships were maintained over long periods. But he undoubtedly expected to receive the same loyalty from colleagues that he gave himself and tended to question the integrity of those who left him or came to question and oppose his strategy.

It is plain that the political differences he had with former comrades in the debates surrounding the formation of a Com-munist Party in 1920-21 were exacerbated by personality clashes of a particularly bitter kind. It is also clear that Maclean played his part in contributing to this atmosphere of personal hostility and general bad feeling. However,in the final analysis, his criticisms of the way the CPGB was created and of those who came, initially, to lead it cannot be dismissed simply as the rantings of an embittered man. Likewise his views on the nature of Bolshevik involvement in the process of that creation as well as the particular role of the 'Hands Off Russia' campaign are worthy of proper consideration.

In many respects Maclean would be more intelligible to those more used to studying the political lives of Bolsheviks than British Social Democrats of the old school or British contemporaries in the C.P. Certainly what is distinctive about Maclean is not his 'Scottishness' but the 'non-Britishness' of his approach to political questions. It is difficult to find a British figure with whom to compare Maclean.If we stretch 'British' to include James Connolly we perhaps have the nearest comparable figure, but even here the comparison is strained. Connolly was not an orthodox Marxist in the way Maclean clearly was and even their approach to Nationalism,on the face of it the most obvious point of connection,was quite different.

It is interesting that while Maclean was an unequivocal supporter of the 1916 Easter Rising in Dublin and acknowledged Connolly's role as a principled socialist revolutionary he never justified his own variant of nationalist politics by reference to Connolly. Moreover his defence of Connolly's participation in an insurrection which virtually all British socialists condemned either in sorrow or outrage was framed in Leninist terms and justified as a major blow against British imperialism. Likewise his defence of Sinn Fein, a body he clearly recognised as nonsocialist was based predominantly on anti-imperialist grounds and we have pointed out that he emphasised to Sinn Feiners the necessity of placing their activities in an Internationalist context.

We have already rehearsed the arguments about Maclean's nationalism but want to state emphatically that it was contingent upon circumstances and was, secondly, subordinate to his over-riding political objective, which was world revolution. In this sense his support for an independent Scotland and creation of the SWRP were contingent upon his desire to remain in a proper relationship with the articles of the Third International and his belief that it was a mechanism for keeping Scotland out of an anticipated war between the British Empire and America. It was not based upon any higher commitment to a concept of nation and did not prevent him working alongside SLP'ers who were notoriously anti-nationalist.

In terms of furthering 'class politics', differences over the idea of Scottish Independence were insufficiently important to prevent co-operation with 'Reds'. Scottish Nationalism, in short, was not the most important issue concerning Maclean even when he had founded the SWRP. It should be noted this is not the same thing as dismissing Maclean's nationalism out of hand or seeing it as a political aberration, a sign of growing political instability, as I. S. McLean suggests. But if contemporary Scottish socialists are looking for guidance from Maclean on an appropriate attitude to adopt towards the national question then there is no automatic advice available. The objective would still have to be approached from a revolutionary internationalist perspective and would be contingent upon how far it contributed to world revolution.

On the wider political front it was because Maclean was so well versed in Marxism that he was able to approach the consequences of the Bolshevik Revolution with a degree of confidence which few of his British contemporaries on the Left could match. It also allowed him to make criticisms of those developments of which he disapproved while maintaining his identification with the Third International. Almost until his death Maclean was able to apply himself to practical political problems with insight and realism. It needs emphasising that Maclean had no direct access to the works of Lenin, Luxemburg nor any of the

Marxist critics of Second International Marxism. Nor had he the ready access to the vibrant intellectual life of continental Marxism. Maclean's politics was developed in a particularly cold intellectual climate, and the fact that he was able to develop his Marxism in ways which brought him close to those more august figures while operating in such isolation is remarkable.

But while he always described himself as a 'Bolshevik' and demonstrated a political approach which in many respects approximates to Bolshevik practice it is dangerous to use such a characterisation too freely. It is pointed out by all commentators on Maclean that he failed to understand the Leninist concept of the revolutionary party. To be more precise he seems to have had no knowledge of the concept; he was ignorant of it, as were all his contemporaries in the revolutionary movement in Britain. It was an idea which never seems to have occurred to him and one which he might have found difficult to accept.

This lack of clear information about a key, perhaps *the* key element of Bolshevik political theory and practice, reflected his general ignorance of the substance of Bolshevism. Like his British contemporaries his commitment to Bolshevism was expressed in terms of unreserved support for the October Revolution. But, unlike them, Maclean had already been developing ideas and strategies which took him on a path away from social democracy and towards the likes of the Bolsheviks and Spartacists before the revolutions in Russia. The connecting point seems to be found in their common preoccupation with interpreting Marxist practice in the era of imperialism and in doing so in a flexible manner. Certainly he was better able than any of his British contemporaries to appreciate something of the flavour of Bolshevism without understanding its full meaning as a development in Marxist thought and political practice.

However, the tendency to look eastwards to Russia for a relevant point of revolutionary connection for someone like

Maclean may blind us to other fruitful lines of inquiry. It may be that the most appropriate comparison is not Lenin and the Bolsheviks but Liebknecht and Luxemburg. They operated within broadly similar economic and social systems and reacted against the failure of Social Democracy in 1914 in similar ways, and while Liebknecht and Luxemburg offered similar enthusiastic support for the Bolshevik revolution, it is doubtful whether they would have approved the way the Bolsheviks subsequently behaved in expelling other socialists from the soviets. Luxemburg's apparent fear that the Bolshevik Party might end up creating a dictatorship over, and not of, the working class came to be shared by one of Maclean's political allies, Peter Petroff, and may have concerned Maclean had he a clearer picture of events in Russia.

Obviously it is impossible to know what criticisms Maclean might have made of Bolshevik theory and practice if he had come to know it more closely. It seems possible, if not certain, that the absence of Maclean, Liebknecht and Luxemburg from the earliest deliberations of the Comintern may have prevented its leaders from developing a more accurate appreciation of the real situation of the revolutionary Left and the range of contrary ideas about revolutionary strategy in the West. Stuart Macintyre has argued that while Lenin came increasingly to believe that Russian experience could be applied to Western countries, 'he retained a sense of caution and uncertainty: he was quite sure that certain approaches were wrong but much less sure that his own recommendations were right . . .'[4]

It is also significant that when Lenin came to review the failure of the revolutionary parties of the West just before his death he criticised the Bolsheviks for underestimating the extent to which Western revolutionaries needed educating in the nature of Bolshevism itself. There were hardly any present who, like Luxemburg, Liebknecht or Maclean, possessed the necessary revolutionary credentials and confidence to at least raise the question about the Bolshevik strategy itself and perhaps ensure that the Comintern developed as a genuine Communist International. But while Luxemburg and Liebknecht were dead, Maclean had the opportunity of being present to correct, at the very least, some of the misleading estimates of the revolutionary potential of British workers in 1920, estimates which clearly misled Lenin. No satisfactory explanation for his failure to make his way to Moscow has ever been given but this was unquestionably a most serious mistake, since the Comintern was a body where Maclean could have expected a sympathetic hearing and where he might have had some effect.

Perhaps finally it is interesting to imagine the legacy which Maclean might have left had he lived longer. What would he have made of the historic debates and struggles taking place within the Comintern, and Soviet Union; debates which seem to have passed by the uncomprehending gaze of most British communists without serious comment? What would he have made of the CPGB's role in the General Strike and the performance of the Labour Governments of 1924 and 1929-31? What, finally, would he have made of the rise of Hitlerism, the emergence of Stalinism and the development of Trotskyism? Certainly, had he lived a normal life-span, Maclean might have found rather more political space in which to emphasise his right to be recognised not as a British or Scottish but as an Internationalist Socialist of real substance.

Abbreviations used in the notes

Notes

Introduction

1 It is difficult to date the starting-point for this renewed interest in Maclean but the publication of Walter Kendall's *The Revolutionary Movement in Britain 1900-21*, London, 1969, certainly acted as a catalyst. Two biographies (John Broom, *John Maclean*, Loanhead, 1973 and Nan Milton, *John Maclean*, London, 1973) carried Maclean to a wider audience, as did Nan Milton (ed.), *In The Rapids of Revolution*, London, 1978, which provided a collection of some of Maclean's articles. Thereafter a considerable number of pamphlets, articles and other forms of publication have focused on Maclean. Most recently D. Howell, *A Lost Left*, Manchester, 1986, has coupled Maclean with James Connolly and John Wheatley, in a study of nationalism and socialism, and Terry Brotherstone has produced a necessarily brief but very stimulating survey of Maclean's political significance in *SLHSJ*, 23, 1988, pp. 15-29. Brotherstone's article is a piece that all interested in Maclean should read.

2. The most important recent study is Iain S. McLean, *The Legend of Red Clydeside*, Edinburgh, 1983. McLean's book, based on his PhD, offers a detailed rebuttal of the idea that Bolshevik or other revolutionary socialist ideas enjoyed widespread support amongst working-class Clydesiders. Christopher Harvie, *No Gods and Precious Few Heroes*, London, 1981, is intellectually and chronologically more wide-ranging but offers a broadly similar approach in demythologising the idea of 'Red' Clydesiders.

3 See, for example, David Kirkwood, *My Life of Revolt*, London, 1935; E. Shinwell, *Conflict Without Malice*, London, 1955; R. K. Middlemas, *The Clydesiders*, London, 1965; John McNair, *James Maxton: The Beloved Rebel*, London, 1955.

4 McNair, *James Maxton*, p. 48.

5 See James MacDougall's dictated reminiscences in the John Maclean Collection, NLS, hereafter MacDougall's reminiscences.

6 See V. I. Lenin, *British Labour and British Imperialism*, London, 1969, pp. 162, 201.

7 See W. Gallacher, *Revolt on the Clyde*, London, 1936, pp.214-15; T. Bell,

180

John Maclean: Fighter For Freedom, Glasgow, 1944, p. 79.

8 McLean, *The Legend*, pp. 144-9.

9 MacDiarmid saw Maclean as the greatest Scotsman since Burns and celebrated him in two poems: *John Maclean (1879-1923),* and *Krassivy, Krassivy.*
See H. MacDiarmid, *Complete Poems 1920-76,* London, 1978. He also
defended Maclean against the allegations of mental instability: H. Mac-
Diarmid, *The Company I've Kept,* London, 1966, p. 139.

10 See Kendall, *Revolutionary Movement,* p. 300-2.

11 See R. Challinor, *The Origins of British Bolshevism,* London, 1977, pp. 246-7.

12 See James D. Young, *SSLHB,* 39, pp. 80-4.

13 See James Hinton, *The First Shop Stewards' Movement,* London, 1973. More
specifically, see Hinton's review of Kendall, *The Revolutionary Movement,* in
SSLHB, 19, pp. 42-9.

14 I. S. McLean, p. 151. See also W. Knox (ed.), *Scottish Labour Leaders 1918-39,*
Edinburgh, 1984, pp. 179-92.

15 See Howell, *Lost Left,* pp. 157-225.

16 *JBS,* 26, 4, p. 487.

17 See McLean, p. 239.

Chapter 1

1 This description of Maclean's family background and early years is largely
derived from the Maclean Collection and Nan Milton, *John Maclean,*
London, 1973, pp. 15-23.

2 See MacDougall's reminiscences.

3 The *Pollokshaw News,* 5 September 1902, Maclean Collection.

4 MacDougall's reminiscences; Milton, *John Maclean,* p. 30; J. Broom, *John
Maclean,* Loanhead, 1973, p. 22.

5 W. Kendall, *The Revolutionary Movement in Britain, 1900-21,* London, 1969,
p. 334, gives 1902 as the date when Maclean joined the SDF.

6 See *Justice,* 9 May 1903 and onwards.

7 *Scottish Co-Operator,* 21 November 1902.

8 *Scottish Co-Operator,* 20 February 1902.

9 Kendall, *Revolutionary Movement,* Ch. 1.

10 R. Challinor, *The Origins of British Bolshevism,* London, 1977, pp. 9-14.

11 *Justice,* 18 April 1903.

12 *Justice,* 25 April 1903.

13 *Justice,* 9 May 1903.

14 *Justice,* 2 April 1904.

15 *Justice*, 30 May, 22 August, 5 September, 12 September 1903.
16 *Scottish Co-Operator*, 23 October 1903.
17 *Justice*, 26 September, 17 October 1903.
18 *Justice*, 28 May 1904.
19 B:oom, *John Maclean*, p. 26.
20 H. Lee and E. Archbold, *Social Democracy In Britain,* London, 1935, pp. 142-3.
21 *Justice*, October 1904.
22 *Justice*, 31 March 1906.
23 For a brief obituary of Nairn see *Scottish Co-Operator*, 10 January 1902.
24 *Scottish Co-Operator*, 29 January 1904.
25 *Scottish Co-Operator*, 9 December 1904.
26 *Scottish Co-Operator*, 23 October 1908.
27 *Scottish Co-Operator*, 31 July 1908.
28 *Justice*, 3 June 1905.
29 MacDougall's reminiscences retailed in Milton, *John Maclean*, p. 32 and Broom, *John Maclean*, p. 23.
30 See Co-Operative Congress Report, 1905.
31 *Ibid.*
32 *Ibid.*, p. 386.
33 See *Justice*, 25 April 1903.
34 See MacDougall's reminiscences.

Chapter 2

1 D. Howell, *A Lost Left*, Manchester, 1986, pp. 161-71.
2 N. Milton, *John Maclean*, London, 1973, p. 33.
3 MacDougall's reminiscences.
4 *Ibid.*.
5 The entry on James MacDougall in W. Knox (ed.), *Scottish Labour Leaders, 1918-39*, Edinburgh, 1984, pp. 170-5.
6 The entry on Peter Petroff by Murdoch, Rodgers and J. J. Smyth in H. Knox, *Scottish Labour Leaders*, pp. 224-30. Additional information was provided by Petroff's daughter Diana Miller, and by information disclosed by the Home Office from the Closed File on Petroff, H.O. 144/17485-7/306431. The file will be available for public inspection on 1 January 2034!
7 W. Gallacher, *Last Memoirs*, London, 1966, p. 73.
8 H. Lee and E. Archbold, *Social Democracy in Britain*, London, 1935, p. 141.
9 *Justice*, 10 August 1907.
10 Maclean Collection.

11 *Justice*, 24 August 1907.
12 *Justice*, 24 August 1907: 'It is our duty to proclaim the Belfast Council immediately responsible ... and the Liberal Government ultimately responsible for the infamous dead.'
13 *Scottish Co-Operator*, 23 August 1907.
14 *Scottish Co-Operator*, 30 August 1907.
15 *Justice*, 26 June 1909.
16 H. Hyndman, *Further Reminiscences*, London, 1912, p. 459.
17 S. Pierson, *British Socialists: The Journey From Fantasy to Politics*, Harvard, 1979, p. 285.
18 *Ibid.*, pp. 254-61.
19 H. Quelch, 'Socialist policy', *New Age*, 1 August 1908. For information on Harry Quelch see John Saville's entry in J. Bellamy and J. Saville (eds.), *Dictionary of Labour Biography*, Vol. VIII, London, 1987, pp. 198-203.
20 *Forward*, 6 August 1910.
21 *Ibid.*.
22 *Ibid.*.
23 K. D. Brown, *Labour and Unemployment 1900-14*, Newton Abbot, 1971, Ch. 4 *passim*.
24 A. W. McBriar, *Fabian Socialism and English Politics 1884-1918*, Cambridge, 1980, pp. 317-18.
25 *Scottish Co-Operator*, 27 December 1907.
26 *Justice*, 4 April 1908.
27 *Ibid.*
28 *Scottish Co-Operator*, 8 January 1909.
29 *Forward*, 13 February 1909.
30 *Ibid.*
31 *Justice*, 29 October 1910.
32 W. Kendall, *The Revolutionary Movement in Britain 1900-21*, London, 1969, Ch. 2.
33 See, for example, The *New Age*, 19 November 1908 and a letter from an ILP delegate, W. Faulkner, 22 April 1909, for indications of unrest in the ILP. The *New Age* was an important vehicle for the expression of views in favour of a more energetic socialist propaganda by the ILP and the possibility of socialist unity along the lines outlined in the text. Grayson's views were carried in its columns on a regular basis.
34 J. Maclean, *The Greenock Jungle*, Glasgow, 1908.
35 *Scottish Co-Operator*, 22, 29 May; 19 June; 10, 31 July; 4, 18 September 1908.

36 S. Macintyre, *A Proletarian Science: Marxism in Britain 1917-33*, Cambridge, 1980.

37 *Justice*, October-November 1907.

38 *Scottish Co-Operator*, 6 March 1908.

39 W. Knox (ed.), *Scottish Labour Leaders, 1918-39*, Edinburgh, 1984, pp.182-3.

40 *Scottish Co-Operator*, 29 April 1910.

41 Scottish Record Office, (SRO) H. H. 16/124, 1 July 1916.

42 *Scottish Co-Operator*, 22 May 1908.

43 *Scottish Co-Operator*, 18 September 1908.

44 *Scottish Co-Operator*, 23 October 1908.

45 *Scottish Co-Operator*, 31 July 1908.

46 *Justice*, 3 October 1908. But note his letter to the *Scottish Co-Operator*, 31 July 1908, where Maclean clearly suggests that the Citizen Army is necessary to defend socialism against the regular army 'dominated by a capitalist Parliament, officials and officers'.

47 *Scottish Co-Operator*, 29 April, 24 June, 12 August 1910.

48 John Broom, *John Maclean*, Loanhead, 1973, p. 35.

49 See MacDougall's reminiscences, which relate that Maclean and an ex-navy man Jim Morton led SDF-organised demonstrations of the unemployed in 1905.

50 *New Age*, 3 October 1908.

51 *Ibid*.

52 Annual Report of The Co-Operative Congress 1910, pp. 383-4. See also *Scottish Co-Operator*, 29 July 1910.

53 *Scottish Co-Operator*, 8 October 1909.

54 *Forward*, 9 July, 6 August, 24 September 1910.

55 Broom, *John Maclean*, p. 38. Also MacDougall's reminiscences.

56 *Socialist Review*, April 1911.

Chapter 3

1 See W. Kendall, *The Revolutionary Movement in Britain 1900-21*, London, 1969, Ch. 5 and Pierson, *British Socialists: The Journey from Fantasy to Politics*, Harvard, 1979, Ch. 5. For a sense of the arguments see *New Leader* and *New Age* 1909-10, for opposite perspectives.

2 See 'Labour and foreign affairs' by A. J. A. Morris in K. D. Brown (ed.), *The First Labour Party*, London, 1985, pp.270-1. See also A. J. A. Morris, *The Scaremongers*, London, 1985, Chs. 8, 13, 16 and 18, for a description of the Blatchford and Hyndman arguments and F. Brockway, *Socialism Over*

Sixty Years, London, 1946, pp. 121-5 for an account of how ILP'ers confronted them.

3 Pierson, *British Socialists*, pp. 276-7

4 See Kendall, *Revolutionary Movement*, p. 52.

5 Maclean Collection.

6 *Justice*, 29 October 1910.

7 *Revolutionary Movement*, p. 52.

8 *Ibid.*, p. 89.

9 See J. Broom, *John Maclean*, Loanhead, 1973, p. 43.

10 *Justice*, 24 February 1912.

11 See Broom, *John Maclean*, p. 39 and N. Milton, *John Maclean*, London, 1973. pp. 49-51.

12 See *Justice*, 1 April 1911.

13 See *Justice*, 15 April 1911.

14 See H. Francis and D. Smith, *The Fed.*, London, 1980, p. 10.

15 See *Justice*, 29 July 1911.

16 *Justice*, 4 January 1913.

17 See W. Knox, *Scottish Labour Leaders, 1918-39*, Edinburgh, 1984, p. 173. Cf. Kendall, *Revolutionary Movement*, p. 354, where he notes a letter to that effect from H. McShane.

18 Maclean Collection.

19 *Justice*, 15 April 1911.

20 *Ibid.*.

21 For an account see Milton, *John Maclean*, pp. 71-2, drawn from Mac-Dougall's reminiscences.

22 *Justice*, 4 October 1913.

23 See *Justice*, 29 October 1914; also J. P. M. Millar, *The Labour College Movement*, London, 1980, p. 20.

24 Annual Co-Operative Conference Report, 1914, p. 474.

25 See *The Scottish Co-Operator*, 1 December 1911.

26 *Ibid.*.

27 *Ibid.*.

28 Annual Co-Operative Conference Report, 1914, p. 491.

29 *Justice*, 10 May 1913.

30 For an estimate of Labour and Socialist strength in Scotland at this time, see W. Hamish Fraser, 'The Labour Party in Scotland', pp. 38-63, in Brown (ed.), *The First Labour Party*.

31 See *Justice*, 25 October 1913.

32 *Justice*, 1 November 1913.
33 See Kendall, *Revolutionary Movement*, p. 61.

Chapter 4

1 FO. 371/3295/20491.
2 *Justice*, 13 August 1914.
3 *Labour Leader*, 24 September 1914.
4 *Labour Leader*, 22 October 1914.
5 See Knox, *Scottish Labour Leaders 1918-39*, Edinburgh, 1984, p. 183.
6 *Justice*, 17 September 1914.
7 See *Scottish Co-Operator*, 5 and 19 November 1915. Maclean was listed with MacDougall as part of the Scottish National Co-Operative Propaganda Campaign and latterly as an active participant at a talk given by Professor Hall (Co-Operative Union Director of Studies) on co-operation and education. Thereafter he is rarely mentioned.
8 See J. Broom, *John Maclean*, Loanhead, 1973.
9 *Scottish Co-Operator*, 13 August 1914.
10 *Justice*, 13 August 1914.
11 See G. R. Rubin, 'The composition of the munitions tribunals in Glasgow during the First World War', *SESH*, 6, p. 49.
12 See *Scottish Co-Operator*, 4 December 1914.
13 See I. S. McLean, *The Legend of Red Clydeside*, Edinburgh, 1983, pp. 55-8.
14 *Ibid.*, Ch. 2; see also J. Melling, 'The Glasgow rent strike and Clydeside labour, *SLHSJ*, 13, pp. 39-44, and J. Melling (ed.), *Housing, Social Policy and The State*, London, 1980, esp. pp. 147-51.
15 See *Labour Leader*, 28 October 1915.
16 *Labour Leader*, 18 November 1915.
17 *Labour Leader*, 25 November 1915.
18 McLean, *Legend*, pp. 25-6.
19 See N. Milton, *John Maclean*, London, 1973, p. 103.
20 The *Vanguard*, December 1915.
21 See in particular McLean, *Legend* and importantly J. Hinton, *The First Shop Stewards' Movement*, London, 1973, pp. 103-70. Much of the detail on the munitions issue on Clydeside is derived from these two studies.
22 See McLean, *Legend*, p. 31.
23 See Lord Askwith, *Industrial Problems and Disputes*, London, 1920, pp. 375-6.
24 See McLean, *Legend*, pp. 28-37 *passim*.
25 See McLean, *Legend*, pp. 35-7.

26 *Labour Leader*, 14 and 28 October 1915, describes the Fairfields dispute and claims the three men initially gaoled, MacPherson, Turner and Fleming, were ILP'ers. For an official view see *History of the Ministry of Munitions*, Vol. 4, pp. 50-65.

27 See G. Rubin *War, Law and Labour*, Oxford, 1987, chs. 5 and 9 *passim*.

28 McLean, *Legend*, p. 47.

29 See Hinton, *Shop Stewards*.

30 W. Kendall, *The Revolutionary Movement in Britain 1900-21*, London, 1969, p. 11.

31 See Milton, *John Maclean*, pp. 108-12.

32 For a fuller description of the Petroff internments see J. McHugh and B. Ripley, 'Russian political internees in First World War Britain – the cases of Peter Petroff and George Chicherin', *HJ*, 1985, pp. 727-38.

33 The *Vanguard*, December 1915.

34 See W. Gallacher, *Revolt on the Clyde*, London, 1936, pp. 60-1.

35 Milton, *John Maclean*, pp. 99-101.

36 Sylvia Pankhurst, *The Home Front*, London, 1987, p.263.

37 For an account of the trial see *Glasgow Herald*, 11 November 1915.

38 See SRO H.H.16/122/26385.

39 Reported in *Justice*, 18 November 1915.

40 *Justice*, 25 November 1915.

41 *Justice*, 9 December 1915.

42 *Scottish Co-Operator*, 10 December 1915.

43 For Maclean's account see Maclean Collection.

44 See McLean, *Legend*, Ch. 5, *passim*.

45 Patterson, letter to Llewellyn Smith, 1 January 1916, Beveridge Collection, Vol. 3, p. 111.

46 According to the Home Office Departmental Record Officer on 4 October 1982, the Internment Order was actually made on 28 January 1916, because his activities and associations were regarded as hostile to this country.

47 *Justice*, 23 December 1915.

48 *Justice*, 30 December 1915.

49 *Justice*, 30 December 1915.

50 This is derived from the 'closed' Chicherin file HO/144/2158/322428. It also contains the point that Maclean was forbidden to correspond with or see any of the 14b internees although he was on Chicherin's list of desired visitors.

51 T. Brotherstone, 'The suppression of the *Forward*, *SLHSJ*, 1969, pp. 2-23. Also J. Hinton, 'The suppression of *Forward* – a note', *SLHSJ*, 1973, pp.4-9.

52 See J. P. M. Millar, *The Labour College Movement*, London, 1980, p. 200.

53 Kendall, *Revolutionary Movement*, pp. 125-7.

54 *Ibid.*.

55 For an acount of the trial see the *Glasgow Herald*, 12 April 1916.

56 G. Rubin, 'A note on the Scottish Office reaction to John Maclean's drugging allegations, *SLHSJ*, 14, pp. 40-5.

57 *Scottish Co-Operator*, 11 November 1910.

58 *CFT*, 28 April 1916.

59 *Ibid.*.

60 Maclean Collection.

61 SRO, H.H.16/123/26385/9.

62 H.H.16/127/26385/8.

63 *CFT*, 12 May 1916. She was also raising the issue of McDougall's health; see *New Age*, 24 August 1916. For a brief biography of Mary Bridges Adams see J. Bellamy and J. Saville (eds.), *Dictionary of Labour Biography*, London, 1984, Vol. VI, pp. 1-7.

64 See H.H.16/127/26385/12.

65 H.H.16/123/26385/15 and 18 dated 1 December 1916 and 14 February 1917.

66 H.H.16/126/26385/20.

67 *Ibid.*

68 H.H.16/123/26385/20.

69 H.H.16/123/26385/24.

70 Lansbury's letter dated 12 June 1917, in H.H.16/123/26385/27.

71 H.H.16/129/26385/35.

72 *Scottish Co-Operator*, 13 July 1917.

73 H.H.16/129/26385/35.

74 H.H.16/124/26385/33.

75 H.H.16/123/26385/20.

76 H.H.16/125/26385/47.

77 *Ibid.*

78 *The Call*, 5 July 1917.

79 *CFT*, 9 November 1917.

80 Chicherin File, /322428/40.

81 *CFT*, 9 November 1917.

82 The *New Statesman*, 1 December 1917, H.H.16/128/26385/39 refers to

M15 interest, quoting filing ref. 241508/M15/F3.

83 Gallacher, *Revolt on the Clyde*, p. 171.

84 Fo/371/3295/20491.

85 H.O./45/318095/673. This file notes a letter from Maclean on his official notepaper concerning the repatriation of Russians. On the front of the file is written 'Not acknowledged'. It then explains the decision not to recognise the 'soi-disant' Russian Consul and discusses the possibility of preventing him using the titles. The Scottish Office noted on the file that it was not thought worthwhile to do anything at present.

86 H.H.16/130/26385/36 and 41.

87 H.H.16/130/26385/42.

88 H.H.16/132/26385/44, dated 15 March 1918.

89 This speech is reprinted in full in T. Brotherstone (ed.), *Accuser of Capitalism*, London, 1986. See also N. Milton (ed.), *In The Rapids of Revolution*, London, 1978, pp. 100-14.

90 *Forward*, 18 May 1918, in McLean, *Legend*, p. 151.

91 V. I. Lenin, *British Labour and British Imperialism*, London, 1969, p. 201.

92 See H.H.16/136/26385, which provides a timetable as follows: 9 May 1918, Maclean refused food. May 10, agreed to accept prison food provided arrangements were made to bring food in from outside and permitted to contact Agnes Maclean to make such arrangements. May 11, complained of food disagreeing with him and refused to take any more; also demands transfer to a Glasgow prison where food can be brought in. May 18, Mrs Maclean apparently failed to arrange for food to be brought in having spent two days trying to make arrangements. July 1 1918, Maclean was now artificially fed and on July 26 Agnes Maclean learns about it and complains.

93 H.H.16/125/26385/51.

94 H.H.16/135/26385/49. He was refused his request to receive the *Economic Journal* and *The Economist* as they were deemed to be current magazines. One official rather sardonically noted that they hardly counted as such. It is clear that if he gave up his protest about food *and* prison work something would be done 'but the Secretary of State cannot entertain it until then'.

95 H.H.16/126/26385/71.

96 See J. Broom, *John Maclean*, London, 1973, pp. 116-17.

97 H.H.16/134/26385/73.

98 c.f. The *Scotsman* and *Glasgow Herald*, both 14 December 1918.

99 J. Vincent (ed.), *The Crawford Papers*, Manchester, 1984, p. 399

Chapter 5

1 S. Macintyre, *A Proletarian Science*, London, 1986, Ch. 5.
2 *Ibid.*, p. 158.
3 See The *Call*, 6 and 13 February 1919, for a flavour of this tour.
4 The *Call*, 23 January 1919.
5 The *Call*, 6 March 1919.
6 The *Call*, 30 January 1919.
7 The *Call*, 27 March 1919.
8 The *Call*, 23 October 1919.
9 The *Call*, 9 October 1919.
10 See W. Kendall, *The Parliamentary Movement in Britain 1900-21*, London, 1969, pp. 201-2.
11 The *Call*, 17 April 1919.
12 The *Call*, 7 February 1918.
13 See Manifesto of the Communist International, April 1919, cited by J. Degras, *Communist International*, London, 1956, Vol. I. p. 4.
14 C. L. Mowat, *Britain Between the Wars*, London, 1955, p. 20.
15 S. R. Graubard, *British Labour and the Russian Revolution 1917-24*, Oxford, 1956, p. 118.
16 Account in Guy A. Aldred, *Communism: Story of the Communist Party*, Glasgow, 1943.
17 J. W. Hulse, in *The Formulation of the Communist International*, Stanford, 1964, p. 117, says: 'during the first five months of the Communist International's existence, her intepretations of the British scene were accepted as authentic by the BCCI and by Lenin. Her articles appeared in the first five numbers of the Communist International in its various language editions.'
18 J. T. Murphy *Preparing for Power*, London, 1934, p. 202.
19 *Workers Dreadnought*, 21 February 1920.
20 J. T. Murphy in The *Socialist*, 6 May 1920.
21 The *Call*, 28 August 1919.
22 The *Call*, 27 November 1919.
23 H. McShane and J. Smith, *No Mean Fighter*, London, 1978, p. 112.
24 J. Walton-Newbold, uncatalogued collection held at Manchester University Library.
25 W. Gallacher, *Last Memoirs*, London, 1966, p. 141.

26 V. I. Lenin, *Collected Works*, Moscow, 1961, Vol. 22, p. 180.

27 For detailed and polemical accounts of Rothstein's 'rightist' political stance, see Kendall, *The Revolutionary Movement*, and R. Challinor, *The Origins of British Bolshevism,* London, 1977.

28 Walton-Newhold, uncatalogued collection.

29 Arthur Upham-Pope, *Maxim Litvinov*, London, 1943, p. 131.

30 R. Bruce-Lockhart, *Memoirs of a British Agent*, London, 1932, p. 199.

31 Walton-Newhold, uncatalogued collection.

32 Basil Thomson, *Queer People*, London, 1927, p. 290.

33 For a full discussion (and defence) of Rothstein, see the introduction by J. Saville in T. Rothstein, *From Chartism to Labourism* (1929), London, 1983.

34 For an account see J. McHugh and B. J. Ripley, 'Russian political internees in First World War Britain', *HJ*, 28, 3, 1985, pp. 727-38.

35 J. Klugmann, *History of the Communist Party of Great Britain*, London, 1969, Vol. I, p. 49.

36 The *Vanguard*, June 1920.

37 The *Vanguard*, December 1920.

38 Entry on Cecil L'Estrange Malone in J. Bellamy and J. Saville (eds.), *Dictionary of Labour Biography*, Macmillan, 1984, Vol. VII, pp. 159-65.

39 The *Worker*, 14 October 1922.

40 Klugmann, *History*, Vol. I, p. 182.

41 See A. Boyle, *The Climate of Treason*, London, pp. 31-3.

42 'Open letter to Lenin', The *Socialist*, 30 January 1921.

43 F. Meynell, *My Lives*, London, 1971, p. 127.

44 *Ibid.*, p. 130. Meynell (later Sir Francis) seems to have had a habit of attempting to use personal acquaintance to escape painful consequences. Arrested at a suffrage meeting in 1911 he says, 'I shouted to sympathetic onlookers that I was a friend of Reginald McKenna, the new Home Secretary', (p. 72).

45 James Hinton, *SSLHB*, 38, p. 68.

46 The *Vanguard*, May 1920.

47 *Ibid.*.

48 Ross was particularly disliked by Gallacher. 'This fellow was one of a number of harpies who were clinging like parasites to John. Up to the last, John got mass support from the working class and, with his public meeetings and Marxist classes, he drew in sufficient money to maintain this ex-policeman and something to spare for two or three others. Strange that with his obsession about spies he should have such a questionable

customer as his constant companion,' W. Gallacher, *Last Memoirs*, pp. 163-6.

49 'The Irish Sinn Feiners who make no profession of socialism or com-munism, and who are at best non-socialists, are doing more to help Russia and the revolution than all we professed marxian Bolsheviks in Britain.' 'Up, India!', The *Vanguard*, August 1920.

50 The *Vanguard*, December 1920.

51 'Open letter to Lenin'.

52 *Communist*, 5 February 1921.

53 Klugmann, *History*, Vol. I, p. 69.

54 T. A. Jackson, *Solo Trumpet*, London, 1953, p. 165. He has an ingenious explanation to offer those who might be deceived by the SLPs continuing publication output. 'You may have come across reprints of these pamphlets, variously priced of a date much later than 1920 – at which time the S.L.P. virtually ceased to exist, being (save for an odd skeleton branch or two) incorporated into the Communist Party. The explanation is that . . . these historic stereotypes passed into the legal possession of the S.L.P. National Executives left stranded by the secession of virtually their entire member-ship – and the practical custody of its sole survivor, the National Secretary. He a die-hard of die-hards, went on issuing from these plates for years after the S.L.P. in practice had dwindled into himself alone.' pp. 148-9.

55 There was some awareness of this problem at the London Unity Conven-tion, 'directly the vote (on Labour Party affiliation) had been taken William Mellor . . . got up and declared that as so serious a decision had been taken, its implementation should be delayed three months in order for its implications to sink in. The result was the reverse . . .' Klugmann, *History*, p. 48, fn.

56 James Hinton, *The First Shop Stewards' Movement*, London, 1973, p. 276.

57 James Clunie, *The Voice of Labour*, Dunfermline, 1958, p. 64.

58 'Open letter to Lenin'.

59 Election address, November 1922.

60 The *Vanguard*, December 1920.

61 McShane and Smith, *No Mean Fighter*, London, 1978, pp. 112-13.

62 Letter to James Clunie, 23 July 1923, cited in James Clunie, *The Voice of Labour*.

63 Guy Aldred, *Communism: Story of the Communist Party*, Glasgow, 1943.

64 I. S. McLean, 'The Labour Movement in Clydeside, Politics, 1914-22', PhD thesis, University of Oxford, November 1977, p. 230.

65 D. Howell, *A Lost Left*, Manchester, 1986, p. 219.

66 McShane and Smith, p. 140.
67 Executive Committee of the Comintern. *Moscow's Reply to the I.L.P.*, May 1920.
68 The *Vanguard*, September 1920.
69 'Open letter to Lenin'.
70 CAB 24/41/3587.
71 Howell, *Lost Left*, p. 223.
72 J. T. Murphy in the *New Reasoner*, Winter 1958/59.

Chapter 6

1 I. S. McLean, *The Legend of Red Clydeside*, Edinburgh, 1983, p. 152.
2 The *Vanguard*, September 1920.
3 The *Call*, 30 January 1919.
4 'Open letter to Lenin', the *Socialist*, 30 January 1921.
5 The *Vanguard*, November 1920.
6 *Ibid*.
7 The *Vanguard*, December 1920.
8 'Let attention be paid to point 17. "Each party must change its old name to that of communist party of such and such country, section of the Third International." William Gallacher is going the rounds ridiculing the idea of a "Scottish" Communist Party because he has been to Russia and poses as the gramophone of Lenin. Nothing in point 17 precludes the formation of a Scottish Party as Scotland is a definite country.' The *Vanguard*, December 1920. (The reference is to the seventeenth point of the twenty-one points of the Theses and Statutes of the Third International).
9 The *Vanguard*, November 1920.
10 The *Vanguard*, December 1920.
11 Report in *Daily Record*, 27 December, 1920.
12 The *Socialist*, 12 May 1921.
13 'Open letter to Lenin'.
14 The *Socialist*, 12 May 1921.
15 *Ibid*.
16 SRO H.H.16/122/26385.
17 *Ibid*.
18 *Ibid*.
19 *Ibid*.
20 *Ibid*.
21 James Clunie, *The Voice of Labour*, Dumfermline, 1958, p. 80.

22 James Clunie was an SLP'er, a full-time tutor at the Scottish Labour College, editor of The *Socialist* during Tom Mitchell's imprisonment and later Labour MP for Dumfermline. In all these capacities, and as a confidant of Maclean, he was a particular object for the wrath of Gallacher and the CPGB. Most of Maclean's correspondence between 1921 and 1923 that was not with his family was with Clunie, who also conveyed Maclean's *'Open letter to Lenin'* to Peter Petroff in Moscow.

23 For McShane's account, see J. Smith and H. McShane, *No Mean Fighter*, London, 1978, p. 140.

24 D. Howell, *A Lost Left*, Manchester, 1986, p. 222.

25 Election address, November 1922, Maclean Collection.

26 Letter to Clunie, 24 November 1922.

27 See J. P. M. Millar, *The Labour College Movement*, London, 1980, pp. 20-1.

28 See Maclean Collection.

29 R. C. Challinor, *The Origins of British Bolshevism*, London, 1977, p. 274. Quoted by J. T. Murphy, *New Horizons*, London, 1941, p. 191.

30 McShane and Smith, p. 150-1.

31 *Forward*, 25 August 1923, cited by Howell, *Lost Left*, p. 224.

32 Howell, *Lost Left*, p. 223.

33 Election address, February 1923, Maclean Collection.

34 Described in *Glasgow Evening Times*, 14 April 1923.

35 J. Broom, John Maclean, Loanhead, 1973, p. 158.

36 For an account, see Comrade Tom Anderson, 'Comrade John Maclean M.A.', pamphlet, Glasgow, 1930.

37 Maclean's own account in letter to James Clunie, 4 June 1923, Maclean Papers, NLS.

38 Letter to Clunie, 30 July 1923, Maclean Papers, NLS.

39 The candidates were as follows: Kinning Park, J. Maclean; Kingston, C Maclean; Townhead, Edward Rennie; Woodside, Allan Hannah; Mile End, Thomas M'Gregor; Gorbals, Norman M'Neil; Govan Central, Peter Marshall; Hutchiesontown, John Ball; Maryhill, Peter M'Intyre; Anderston, Alexander Shane; Cowcaddens, Frank Shevlin; Calton, Thomas Hitman.

40 The *Worker*, 6 October 1923.

41 SWRP leaflet, 'October 1923, Maclean Collection.

42 S. Pankhurst, letter in Maclean Collection.

43 Election address, 23 November 1923, Maclean Collection.

44 *Ibid*.

45 Election leaflet, November 1923, Maclean Collection.

46 *Ibid.*
47 The *Commune*, December 1923.

Chapter 7

1 D. Howell, *A Lost Left,* Manchester, 1986, p. 224.
2 I. S. McLean, 'The Labour Movement in Clydeside Politics, 1914-22', PLD thesis, University of Oxford, November 1977, p. 234.
3 John Mitchell, review of R. K. Middlemas, *The Clydesiders in Scottish Vanguard*, June 1968.
4 The 1931 candidates were: Govan, Edward Rennie; Cowcaddens, B. Evans; Fairfield, Joseph P. Vincent; Paisley, R. Carlton. In the third ward R. Carlton came third of five candidates, with more than 240 votes.
5 Hulchiesontown – Peter M'Intyre.
6 The by-law forbidding public meetings on the Green had been passed in 1916 but not applied after the war until 1924. The SWRP defied the ban alongside, but independently of, Guy Aldred's Anti-Parliamentary Communist Federation. W. Gallacher, in *The Worker*, called the opposition 'a stunt pure and simple'. J. T. Caldwell, 'Guy Aldred, Anti-Parliamentarian, 1886-1963: A Memoir', in *Essays in Scottish Labour History,* ed. I. Macdougall, Edinburgh, 1978.
7 Tom Anderson: 'Class-conscious notes', The *Scottish Workers' Republic*, 18, March 1929.
8 The *Scottish Workers' Republic*, 2, September 1927.
9 *Manifesto of the Scottish Workers' Republican Party,* 1925.
10 The *Scottish Workers' Republic,* 5, January 1928.
11 *Ibid.*
12 James Clunie, *The Voice of Labour,* Dumfermline, 1958.
13 Nan Milton, *In the Rapids of Revolution,* London, 1978; *John Maclean,* London, 1973, and, 'John Maclean and Scottish independence,' pamphlet published by John Maclean Society.
14 James Hinton, review note on *In the Rapids of Revolution*, *SSLHB*, 39, Spring 1979.
15 Howell, *Lost Left*, p. 216.
16 Cited by J. Broom, *John Maclean,* Loanhead, 1973, p. 154.
17 I. S. McLean, *The Legend of Red Clydeside*, Edinburgh, 1983, p. 151.
18 The first public declaration appears to have been in The *Vanguard*, September 1920.
19 Milton, 'John Maclean and Scottish independence'.

20 The *Socialist*, December 1922.

21 *Ibid*.

22 N. Milton, *In the Rapids of Revolution,* London, 1978, p. 163.

23 Milton, 'John Maclean and Scottish independence'.

24 Letters to James Clunie, Maclean Papers, NLS.

25 *Ibid*.

26 *Ibid*.

27 *Ibid*.

28 James D. Young, 'John Maclean's place in Scottish history' *SSLHB*, 39, pp. 80-4.

29 Hugh McDiarmid, *The Company I've Kept*, London, 1966, p. 151.

Conclusion

1 See T. Brotherstone, 'John Maclean and the Russian Revolution: a discussion article', *SLHSJ*, 23, pp. 15-29.

2 See Graham Bain, *John Maclean: His Life & Work 1919-23*, Glasgow, 1986.

3 R. K. Middlemas, *The Clydesiders*, London, 1965, p. 50.

4 Macintyre, *A Proletarian Science*, London, 1986, p. 228.

Index

Index